PURCHASE MADE POSSIBLE BY

GOVERNOR ZELL MILLER'S
READING INITIATIVE

1998

D1158172

Florida

The Natural Wonders

Jeff Ripple

Foreword by Clay Henderson
President, Florida Audubon Society

Voyageur Press

Dedication

For Mom and my sisters, Jennifer and Jill

Acknowledgments

As with any book endeavor, there are a number of people whose assistance with this project has meant the difference between its success and failure. I am indebted to Dr. Peter Pritchard and Clay Henderson of the Florida Audubon Society; Dr. Todd Engstrom, Dr. Leonard Brennan, and the staff at Tall Timbers Research Station; Ann Johnson of Florida Natural Areas Inventory; Drs. Mark Deyrup and Eric Menges of the Archbold Biological Station; Dr. Paul Gray of the National Audubon Society, Kissimmee Prairie Preserve; Dick Franz and Dr. David Webb, Florida Museum of Natural History; Randy Tate of The Nature Conservancy, Florida Keys; Debra Nordeen, Alan Scott, and Roberta D'Amico, Everglades National Park; Deb Jansen, Big Cypress National Preserve; and Mark Ludlow, Florida Caverns State Park. They have shared their knowledge and reviewed drafts of chapters. Susan Cerulean and Peter Pritchard accepted the daunting task of reviewing the entire manuscript, for which I am deeply grateful. Thanks to Joe Durando, who helped me identify plants in the transparencies used in this book. I would also like to thank the Florida Division of Recreation and Parks for granting me a permit to photograph in the state parks, as well as the many other people who have been generous with their time and advice. This is my third book with Voyageur Press, and I must thank Tom Lebovsky, Michael Dregni, Todd Berger, Jeni Henrickson, and the rest of the staff for their hard work and the opportunity to publish books with them. Finally, I cannot forget my wife, Renée, for her unflagging support and patience, her advice and humor and company. Thank you, my love.

Page 1: *Gentle waves from the Atlantic wash the shoreline at sunrise, Canaveral National Seashore.*
Facing page: *Hundreds of sabal palms curve toward the sun in this swamp at Merritt Island National Wildlife Refuge.*

Edited by Michael Dregni
Designed by Andrea Rud
Printed in Hong Kong

97   98   99   00   01   5   4   3   2   1

Library of Congress Cataloging-in-Publication Data
Ripple, Jeff, 1963–
    Florida : the natural wonders / by Jeff Ripple
      p. cm.
    Includes bibliographical references (p. 140) and index.
    ISBN 0-89658-324-4
    1. Florida—Description and travel. 2. Natural history—Florida.
    3. Florida—Pictorial works. I. Title.
    F316.2.R47 1997
    508.759—dc20   96-35226
                       CIP

Distributed in Canada by Raincoast Books, 8680 Cambie Street, Vancouver, B.C. V6P 6M9

Published by Voyageur Press, Inc.
123 North Second Street, P.O. Box 338, Stillwater, MN 55082 U.S.A.
612-430-2210, fax 612-430-2211

Please write or call, or stop by, for our free catalog of natural history publications. Our toll-free number to place an order or to obtain a free catalog is 800-888-WOLF (800-888-9653).

Educators, fundraisers, premium and gift buyers, publicists, and marketing managers: Looking for creative products and new sales ideas? Voyageur Press books are available at special discounts when purchased in quantities, and special editions can be created to your specifications. For details contact the marketing department.

Portions of this book appeared in different form in *Earth* and *Birder's World* magazines.

Facing page: *Red mangroves and oyster bars rim Chokoloskee Bay in the Ten Thousand Islands on the Gulf Coast.*

Table of Contents

Foreword

There is a gap between the time you fall in love with Florida and when you truly begin to appreciate the state's natural wonders. Florida is a complex living creature, and subtlety is its most endearing quality. The state possesses great treasures including the Everglades, coral reefs, clear springs, and magnificent forests. It also conceals small jewels, such as tropical tree snails, torreya trees, and wild rosemary. And Florida has a soul.

Deer Island, one of many coastal islands within the Lower Suwannee National Wildlife Refuge, along the Nature Coast (Big Bend) region of the Gulf Coast.

The search for Florida's soul is the adventure of a lifetime. Seek it in the tropical hammocks of Big Pine Key with its spectrum of wild orchids. Maybe you can see it from the dizzying heights of the Apalachicola bluffs. Perhaps it is hidden in the moving shadows below Looe Key on North America's largest coral reef. It could be guarded by alligators in the lettuce lakes of Corkscrew Swamp Sanctuary. Perhaps it is beneath the boil in a place called Blue Spring. In theory, it is the imaginary line near the horizon where the sheen of Florida Bay reflects the image of the sky. But it could also be beyond the idyllic sands of Topsail Hill. Finding the soul of Florida is a search for its special places. Only in that personal discovery can one unlock the subtle mysteries of the natural attraction of Florida.

I have a wonderful job at the Florida Audubon Society. Working with Florida's oldest conservation organization, I get to seek out those special places left in Florida and find ways to protect them for the enjoyment of future generations. For nearly one hundred years, the Audubon Society has been working to protect special places long before they became national parks, wildlife refuges, or state parks. National Audubon Society wardens were protecting wading birds at Flamingo four decades before it became Everglades National Park. Ours is an easy job description: "Saving what's left." It's just that the job gets harder as Florida's population continues to grow.

Unfortunately, Florida is still cannibalizing its fragile natural environment as urban sprawl continues at an alarming pace. With seven hundred or so new Floridians each day, we are destroying native ecosystems and displacing rare species. Ninety percent of our longleaf pine ecosystem is gone. Half of our wetlands have been ditched or drained. Each day bulldozers destroy more scrub, one of our most diverse habitats. Every day more of the Everglades is converted to agriculture or residential development. More than 90 percent of the wading birds that graced our state at the turn of the century are but a memory. Loss of critical habitat means that Florida now has more than two hundred species listed on federal or state lists as endangered, threatened, or of special concern. While most Floridians are aware of the threats to the bald eagle, manatee, and panther, few are sympathetic to the plight of the beach mouse or the Atlantic salt marsh snake. A recent survey by Defenders of Wildlife noted that Florida in general, and south Florida in particular, is now the most endangered landscape in North America.

It is truly staggering how fast this transformation has occurred. In my lifetime the population of this state has quadrupled. A recent report by the University of Florida projects our population will double again in the next twenty years. Yet the past seems like yesterday. My grandmother once took me to the place she was born—a log cabin built by her grandfather on the Withlacoochee River. My father rode horseback on Florida's open range at a time when there were more cattle than people. My mother still talks about her first trip to Miami—a three-day journey along the Old Dixie Highway, a red-brick, tree-canopied road. No place in America has undergone this kind of urban transformation in such a short period of time.

With this change there has been the loss of something almost as precious as the land itself. It is a loss of sense of place. Many people now think of "Florida," the name that derived from "feast of flowers," as a tacky, cluttered, overbuilt, artificial monument to urban sprawl.

But there is good news. Floridians, divided by geography and culture, are united in their love for its outdoors. We connect with our special places. Poll after poll shows that Floridians' fervor for protection of the natural environment equals their concern for family and religion. Protection of Florida's environment has now risen to the level of a fundamental value, and it is natural that people will protect what they value and love.

Florida's conservation ethic has translated into major public policy victories. In 1990, Governor Bob Martinez convinced the Florida Legislature to commit to a ten-year, $3-billion program called Preservation 2000 and committed to save the "best of Florida before it's too late." Preservation 2000 now has important bipartisan support from legislators across the state to acquire new preserves and additions to our state parks, forests, and wildlife management areas. It also funds rails-to-trails, urban greenspace, and greenways. What's even better is that twenty Florida counties that make up the majority of our state's population have voted to tax themselves to produce another $600 million in matching funds to enhance Preservation 2000. The result is the largest program of conservation lands acquisition in the world. More than 600,000 acres of wild Florida lands have already been acquired. With three years left in this decade-long commitment, there is little question that more than one million acres of Florida conservation lands will be protected for future generations.

Other special places, previously exploited for their natural resources, are now the focus of environmental restoration on an historic scale. Congress has approved the restoration of the Kissimmee River, which was channelized for flood control. A monument marks the site near the Oklawaha River where President Lyndon B. Johnson set off the first explosion that began the Cross Florida Barge Canal; a generation later, Governor Lawton Chiles and the Cabinet have begun the process of removing the dikes and dams that will transform the Cross Florida Barge Canal into the Cross Florida Greenway. President Bill Clinton has endorsed and Congress has begun to respond to the most ambitious environmental restoration program ever conceived—the Everglades Restoration. The 1996 Florida Legislature even made the down payment toward the restoration of Lake Apopka, which is so polluted that its lifeless color can be distinguished in satellite photographs. These monumental efforts testify that more environmental restoration work is underway in Florida than in any other place in the world.

Florida's conservation groups continue to play an important part. The Everglades Restoration Campaign was initiated by the National Audubon Society. The important work of land acquisition is carried out for the most part by The Nature Conservancy and the Trust for Public Land. Community groups such as local land trusts and environmental learning centers find ways to educate the public about our ecosystems and focus public resources to protect special places. Florida Audubon Society, like other groups, has grown more professional in its approach to advocacy, education, and science. It works hard to educate public officials on important public policy issues. Together, Florida's conservation groups can provide a vision for what we must do to protect this fragile place we call home.

The time has come to stitch together a new sense of place for Florida. In the next five years, the Florida legislature will examine closely all of Florida's conservation lands and provide answers to the following questions: What have we already acquired or restored? What will we be able to acquire in the final three years of Preservation 2000? What will we not be able to acquire? Can we work with those private land owners to reach land protection agreements, conservation easements, or the like? We must then look at the hard science to see what endangered ecosystems, unique geological features, world-class waterways, and globally imperiled springs should be protected for future generations. We call this a Conservation Plan for Florida. It will be a greenprint for our future.

As I mentioned before, all Floridians are united by their love for the state's special natural places. What divides us is not thinking of ourselves as Floridians. The future of the state is in our hands, and it is up to Floridians to save the natural Florida, upon which so much of our economic health and quality of life depends. Time is running out.

In the pages of this book, Jeff Ripple shares some of the secrets that make Florida a unique and beautiful place. The book provides words and images that offer a starting point toward closing the gap in people's minds between the Florida that we love, but are losing, and the Florida we must understand and protect. It is not enough to love Florida; we must have the knowledge to protect what we love. Once we *know* Florida, perhaps we will be better equipped to address the challenge of preserving our natural heritage. Perhaps then we may regain our lost sense of place.

Clay Henderson
President
Florida Audubon Society

Slash pine and rosemary dominate this coastal scrub in the Florida Panhandle, Gulf Islands National Seashore.

Preface

Four years ago, my wife and I fled the congestion and concrete of south Florida and headed north toward Gainesville, about an hour south of the Florida-Georgia border. Twenty-five miles outside the city, we found a small house with a huge screened porch (for the cats) on eight acres of rosemary, oaks, and longleaf pine (for us). We have few human neighbors. It is quiet, and we have a multitude of birds, squirrels, opossums, raccoons, lizards, snakes, and other creatures that either reside on our acreage or pass through with some regularity. On summer nights, I sit on the steps and watch the fireflies rise from the grass and float up through the trees. Chuck-will's-widows chant from the woods around me. Last night, a gray fox walked out of the woods as I was writing in my office and looked at me through the window before loping away. I am at home here in this house, in these woods, surrounded by my wild acquaintances.

Paintbrush, deer tongue, and goldenrod dominate this display of fall wildflowers among saw palmetto on a recently burned pine flatwoods in the Lower Suwannee National Wildlife Refuge.

I have a hard time grasping the idea of owning this land, so instead I consider myself only its caretaker, under the employ of the wildlife. Their demands are small—a few seeds, a nest box or two, a promise to conduct a prescribed burn, and a guarantee to chase away stray cats, dogs, and pigs. It is a small price to pay for such good company.

Over the past three years, I have traveled to many of Florida's wilderness places in state parks, national parks and forests, national wildlife refuges, and private preserves while writing this book. I have experienced firsthand the diversity and beauty of this state, from the Panhandle beaches to the Keys. On rare occasions, I was allowed brief entrance into the lives of some of its wildlife residents. I have become painfully aware of the vulnerability of the landscape and the isolation of many of its wild remnants. The human touch is everywhere. But the whole of Florida's wilderness is greater than the sum of its parts. This land has a hold on me like no other place.

I first discovered my connection to Florida, my sense of place, in the Everglades and Big Cypress Swamp in the late 1980s. The expanse of the cypress prairies and marshes, at once sweeping and intimate, gave me reason to stay in Florida when the cities had long since convinced me it was time to move on. It was from the Everglades and Big Cypress Swamp that I found my voice, through writing and photography, and it is from these lands that I continue to draw my inspiration.

The details of how Florida's landscape has been savaged and continues to be savaged could easily fill an entire volume. But that is not my purpose here. Instead, I want to celebrate with you in this book what remains of Florida's natural landscape and wildlife. I want to tell you the story of how they came to be, and why I believe they are worth saving. I hope to provide you with a reference from which you can begin your personal journey of discovery, your own search for a sense of place.

Notes on the Photographs

The photographs in this book were created using large-format and 35mm cameras. The large-format camera is a Calumet Woodfield XM 4x5, with 75mm and 90mm lenses. This camera was used to photograph the majority of the landscapes. My 35mm cameras include a Canon AE-1 and Canon F-1, with lenses ranging from 28mm to 300mm. My only filters are 81A warming filters that remain on the lenses at all times and a polarizing filter. Fuji transparency films were used for virtually all of the photographs because of their ability to render sharp detail and accurately reproduce the colors I find in nature. I am grateful for the contributions of photographs by Doug Perrine, Larry Lipsky, John Moran, Dave Maehr, and Barry Mansell, who were able to gather images of essential Florida scenes that I could not.

First Impressions

Lightning splintered the darkness above me as I stepped out of my truck into a marsh along Turner River Road in Big Cypress National Preserve. Garish, neon fingers of electricity carved an erratic path across the night sky, some bolts stalking others from cloud to cloud in a high-voltage game of cat and mouse. Frogs yelped, barked, and grunted, punctuating the continuous rolling thunder and rustling of cordgrass in the fitful breeze. There was no rain, but the thunderstorm to the west was moving closer. A half hour before, I was nearly swallowed by the storm while recording thunder and frogs in Fakahatchee Strand. Twin bolts of lightning struck near the truck an instant before the air exploded around me. The first heavy drops of rain hastened my retreat toward Big Cypress, where I hoped to set up and record again.

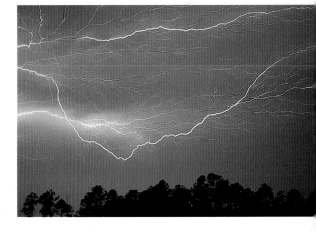

Facing page: *Dahoon holly and Virginia willow line the banks of the spring-fed Ichetucknee River in north Florida. Tape grass waves in the river's cool, clear flow. Clear spring water combined with low acidity and constant, moderate temperatures create conditions ideal for aquatic plants, including tape grass, giant cutgrass, southern naiads, and chara. The plants provide homes to dozens of species of fish, turtles, snakes, mollusks, and insects. The Ichetucknee River runs only six miles before it empties into the Santa Fe River, a major tributary of the Suwannee River.*
Above: *Cloud-to-cloud lightning blazes across the sky during a thunderstorm over Fakahatchee Strand State Preserve in southwest Florida's Big Cypress Swamp.*

Now, five miles away, on the eastern edge of the storm, I felt safe enough to wade deeper into the marsh, recording equipment in hand. Nickle-sized squirrel tree frogs were everywhere, calling in a mating frenzy, their plump bodies bloated with air and passion, big black eyes peering up from the blades of grass when I shone my headlamp down upon them. Standing quietly, I watched the needles of the old sound recorder bounce as the intensity of frog song and thunder ebbed and flowed around me. The night seemed timeless. It was easy for me to imagine this place several thousand years before, when the ocean had only recently retreated from the limestone bedrock beneath my feet, when the first cypress trees were small saplings, when no human had yet to listen to this swamp's thunder and orchestra of frogs.

This was a night Archie Carr would have liked. "There are still remnants of the old wild Florida," he writes in *A Naturalist in Florida*. "There is always something. Anytime. Day or night, cold or warm, in the rain or shining sun you can find bits of the old wild left around. . . ." The late Dr. Carr, an eminent naturalist and sea turtle scientist, effused over a Florida most people never see—the wild Florida. He also seemed at least cautiously optimistic about Florida's ability to survive, in some form, the degradations of an expanding human population and its renourished beaches, oceanfront condos, country club communities, and shopping malls. I share his enthusiasm for Florida's wild places, and I believe we can save many of them for future generations.

"The Feast of Flowers"

Named for the Spanish "feast of flowers," Florida stretches more than four hundred miles from north to south, and nearly as many miles from east to west. The state encompasses the range of 425 species of birds, 3,500 plants, and 65 snakes. It is remarkably flat, especially in south Florida, rising no higher than 230 feet above sea level. More than 1,700 rivers flow through Florida, while some 7,800 natural lakes dimple the state's interior, including Lake Okeechobee, the second largest lake in the continental United States. Florida has nearly 1,350 miles of coastline, more than any state except Alaska. The Florida Natural Areas Inventory distinguishes eighty-one different natural communities in Florida, ranging from beach dunes to tidal swamps. No state east of the Mississippi River can match Florida for its diversity of living things and natural systems.

What gives Florida its remarkable diversity? A warm, humid climate, due in part to the maritime influence of the Caribbean Sea and Gulf of Mexico, certainly helps. Abundant rainfall and the length of the state, which spans six-and-one-half degrees of latitude, are also important. All of these contribute to a remarkable blending of temperate and tropical life forms. Most of Florida's wildlife is of temperate origin, although in south Florida and in the Keys there are several species of tropical invertebrates and many birds from the West Indies and the Bahamas. Tropical trees and understory vegetation dominate in the southern half of the state, with tropical understory plants extending into northern Florida beneath a canopy of temperate trees.

Climate: From Temperate to Tropical

The Florida peninsula protrudes like a giant paw into the warm waters of the Gulf of Mexico and Atlantic Ocean. Because the peninsula is surrounded by warm water, it has not become desert like many other land masses at the same latitude, such as northern Mexico or the Sahara Desert. Instead, Florida's climate ranges from temperate in north Florida to tropical in extreme south Florida and the Keys, with the southern portion of the state experiencing a marked wet season of May through October and a dry season of November through April.

Florida averages forty to fifty-five inches of rain annually—most falling in the summer from afternoon thunderstorms. These thunderstorms produce tumultuous downpours and frequent lightning. More lightning strikes occur in Florida than anywhere else in the world except certain areas of Australia.

Late fall through early spring is typically dry throughout the state, although the northern half can receive significant rainfall from cold fronts pushing down from the north. The amount of rain decreases as the fronts move into the central and southern parts of the peninsula. After a cold front has pushed through, freezing conditions sometimes occur in the Panhandle and northern Florida, while

A wood stork feeds in Mrazek Pond, Everglades National Park. Unlike egrets, herons, and most other wading birds, the wood stork does not rely on vision to catch its typical prey of small fish, frogs, and other similar prey. Instead, it walks slowly through the water, occasionally stirring the bottom mud with its feet, and snaps up any small creature that bumps against its long, stout, but extremely sensitive, beak.

temperatures may dip into the lower forties in central and southern parts of the state. Regardless of how cold the north wind blows, temperatures in the Keys rarely sink below the lower fifties.

The Bermuda high, a semipermanent high-pressure system centered over Bermuda and the Azores in the north Atlantic Ocean, has a profound influence on Florida's weather. In late spring and summer, the Bermuda high is weak, allowing afternoon thunderstorms to develop. From fall through early spring, the location and size of the cell diminishes the chance of rain in Florida by inhibiting cloud formation. It is because of the Bermuda high that the state is not drenched by thunderstorms throughout the year.

The Bermuda high is also partially responsible for the severe spring droughts that occasionally beset Florida. A drought can occur when the Bermuda high expands and drifts close to the eastern United States, creating warm, dry conditions. If the cell lingers and does not weaken, the drought may last well into summer.

Prevailing winds over the state are affected by the Bermuda high as well. Its normal spring and summer position and clockwise rotation trigger a prevailing wind that blows from the southeast over peninsular Florida and from the southwest over north Florida and the Panhandle. If the Bermuda high drifts to the south of its normal position, the prevailing wind over all of Florida is from the southwest. The prevailing wind is overlaid on local winds, such as the onshore sea breeze, and interaction between the prevailing wind and local winds influences local weather. For example, in southeast Florida, where the prevailing wind is normally from the southeast, as is the sea breeze, the combined force of the two help push developing clouds away from the coast. A line of showers often occurs where the breeze from the east coast encounters the sea breeze from the west coast, generally over the Everglades and Big Cypress Swamp. However, if the prevailing wind is from the southwest, then the sea breeze is unable to carry clouds inland, and the result is coastal thunderstorms.

Hurricanes and Tropical Storms

June through November is hurricane season in Florida. Tropical waves (large, weakly organized areas of thunderstorms) move off the western coast of Africa and begin their journey of several thousand miles across the Atlantic and Caribbean Sea. Some die out, but others continue to strengthen as they drift west and become tropical depressions (defined as having wind speeds less than 39 miles per hour). If conditions remain favorable for strengthening, tropical depressions can develop into tropical storms with wind speeds of 39–74 mph and hurricanes with wind speeds greater than 74 mph. The peak time for hurricanes is September and October, when humidity is consistently high and ocean temperatures are at their warmest.

High winds (which can reach sustained speeds of

Fog hangs heavy over a freshwater marsh draped with spider webs in Big Cypress National Preserve. The slash pines in the distance indicate the presence of limestone outcrops that provide slightly higher ground on which the pines and other species needing drier conditions can survive. In Florida, a difference in elevation of only a few inches is all that separates many uplands from lowlands.

more than 150 mph) and flooding caused by the storm surge, heavy rain, and storm-driven waves and tides cause the greatest damage during hurricanes. Islands can be torn in half, thousands of acres of mangrove swamp destroyed, pine forests leveled, and hammocks of giant tropical hardwoods shredded. Coastlines are eroded and dune systems erased.

In spite of the damage hurricanes can cause, natural communities in Florida evolved with hurricanes and recover with time, provided we give them the chance. In fact, much of the diversity of Florida's plant life is a result of hurricanes. Hurricanes are thought to have transported many of the tropical plants found in Florida from the Yucatan Peninsula and the West Indies, washing them ashore with waves or bearing their seeds aloft on high winds. Hurricane winds blow down large trees in hardwood hammocks, fostering an explosion of new plant life on the forest floor that vigorously competes for the extra light and nutrients resulting from the tear in the forest canopy. Florida Bay depends on periodic hurricanes to mix nutrient-rich waters and help regulate the bay's salinity.

Geology

A warm, shallow sea covered Florida through nearly all of its early natural history. The oldest land in the state dates back to the late Oligocene Epoch twenty-five million years ago, while the youngest land—the southwest coast—has been exposed above sea level for only a few thousand years. Geologically speaking, Florida possesses some of the youngest terrain in North America; even its oldest land is relatively recent compared to ancient landscapes such as the Smoky Mountains, which have been around for more than 200 million years and contain sediments nearly a billion years old.

The limestone bedrock beneath Florida is a product of shallow seas that nurtured a plethora of marine organisms whose shells and skeletal remains settled to the ocean floor over the course of millions of years. This limestone was carved by erosive forces during periods when it was exposed to air and then smoothed over by the deposition of new sediments when it was submerged. Vestiges of Florida's marine heritage are evident everywhere; the highest ridges were once coastal dunes, and virtually all major rock

Horseshoe crabs mating and laying eggs on a marl beach edging Florida Bay in Everglades National Park. The horseshoe crab is an arachnid and more closely related to spiders and mites than crabs, which are crustaceans. Female horseshoes come ashore on spring tides (those high tides that occur near the time of the full moon), often with three or four male horseshoes stretched behind her in a chain, each attached to the other, with only the first male actually riding the back of the female. The female buries herself in the sand to lay her eggs, with the males jostling for position on top. Often, a stretch of beach will be covered with hundreds of horseshoe crabs at a time.

Above: *A rare snowfall blankets a creek tumbling into the Suwannee River in north Florida. The temperature in the Panhandle and north Florida can dip below 20°F after a winter cold front passes through. (Photo © John Moran)*
Right: *Sunset spreads warm color across the clouds and dunes on a winter day at St. Joseph Peninsula State Park.*

formations contain marine sediments.

The entire state lies on the Atlantic Coastal Plain, and what land we see exposed today is actually only a sliver of a much broader, flat platform known as the Floridan Plateau. The Floridan Plateau extends to the edge of the continental shelf, beyond which ocean depths plummet to the deep waters of the Atlantic and the Gulf of Mexico. On the east coast, the continental shelf ends fairly close to the shore, while on the west coast, you can travel more than forty miles offshore before encountering deep water.

Florida has not always been a part of North America. Through the Paleozoic Era 600 million to 300 million years ago, the basement rock beneath Florida was part of Africa when that continent was part of a much larger "supercontinent"—Gondwanaland. When Gondwanaland broke apart at the end of the Paleozoic Era, Florida was one of several slabs of continent set adrift in the newly formed Atlantic Ocean. Florida's continental rock drifted for some eighty million years until it finally meshed with the North American continent in the early Mesozoic Era 220 million years ago. South Florida even experienced volcanic activity at one time when an oceanic hotspot developed where the Bahamas are now.

Climatic oscillation and the rise and fall of sea

levels as a result of Ice Ages have dramatically influenced Florida's climate and the size of its landmass since its definitive emergence from the sea twenty-five million years ago. During the Ice Ages, the global climate cooled, polar caps expanded, and immense fields of ice ground their way south to cover much of North America and Europe. Sea levels fell worldwide. Interglacial intervals, or global warming trends, caused glaciers to retreat, polar caps to shrink, and sea level to rise.

During interglacial intervals, the Florida peninsula was much smaller than it is now due to the higher sea level. When the sea was high, most of the state, especially the southern portion, was covered by ocean. Conversely, the peninsula nearly doubled its present size during the peak of the Wisconsin glaciation approximately twenty thousand years ago, when sea level was more than three hundred feet lower than today. Scientists believe Florida at that time was semi-arid and much cooler. Surface water was scarce. The northern half of the peninsula was dominated by dry savannas, with mesic forests occupying moist sites, while the southern half was covered by scrub and sandhill communities.

Early Natural History

Scientists have been able to tell much about Florida's ancient landscape from pollen and vertebrate fossil evidence. According to S. David Webb in his chapter on historical biogeography in *Ecosystems of Florida*, this record indicates that mixed hardwood forest is the oldest terrestrial natural community in Florida, dating back to the first emergence of what is now central Florida twenty-five million years ago. Sandhill and scrub habitats formed about twenty million years ago, while extensive dune systems began to develop during the middle and late Miocene fifteen million years ago. Longleaf pine habitats evolved during the early Pleistocene less than two and a half million years ago. Most swamps, bay-heads, and lakes are no more than a few thousand years old.

Florida is especially rich in fossils from the Cenozoic Era, particularly the Miocene, Pliocene, and Pleistocene Epochs from twenty million to ten thousand years ago. Fossil deposits in what were freshwater areas during the late Miocene have revealed chicken turtles, softshell turtles, garfish, and alliga-

tors. Estuaries were filled with sharks, whales, dugongs (a type of sea cow now found only in the Indian and western Pacific Oceans), and other estuarine and marine creatures. Many birds and browsing ungulates such as peccaries, tapirs, and giraffe-camels lived in Florida's late Miocene forests. Wildlife that roamed the subtropical savannas included cranes, giant tortoises, an extinct pronghorn antelope, two kinds of camels and rhinoceroses, and by the end of the Miocene, ten species of horses. New immigrants to Florida included sabercats and primitive bears from the Old World, as well as two species of South American ground sloths. The first relatives of elephants also showed up during the late Miocene, including the American mastodon and the shovel-tusker, named for a pair of large, flattened tusks that it used like shovels.

Subtropical savannas and forests persisted in Florida throughout much of the Pliocene even as other areas in North America became more arid. This habitat allowed many grazing and browsing animals to survive in Florida when they had already disappeared elsewhere on the continent. Among these animals were a few species of horses, peccaries, and a type of llama.

After the formation of the Isthmus of Panama two and a half million years ago, Florida experienced what is known as the "great American interchange" of animals with Central and South America. Near the end of the Pliocene, several immigrants from South America found their way to Florida, including a giant, flightless predatory bird, *Titanis*, that stood more than nine feet high; a relative of the modern South American capybara; and three different kinds of

huge ground sloths that ranged in size from bear to elephant. Among the many other species of creatures that walked, flew, slithered, or swam to Florida from South America were an extinct porcupine, the manatee, a vampire bat, several species of snakes, and a glyptodont—a large, thick-shelled armadillo-like creature. Animals of North American origin also migrated to South America through Mexico and Central America—tapirs, peccaries, llamas, horses, sabercats, raccoons, spectacled bears, and jaguars.

During the early Pleistocene, an extensive subtropical savanna fringed the Gulf of Mexico linking Florida to western North America and to Central and South America. As a result, Florida shared many species of mammals, birds, reptiles, and plants with arid western regions. By the mid-Pleistocene, the semi-arid corridor around the Gulf of Mexico is thought to have broken, isolating many Florida species of xeric or dry-climate reptiles, birds, and plants from their western relatives. The Florida scrub jay,

burrowing owl, gopher tortoise, indigo snake, and many of Florida's cacti became relicts that survive to this day in rare, arid habitats such as scrub in central Florida and in a few areas on the Atlantic and Gulf coasts.

The Asian long-horned bison, the ancestor of today's North American bison, arrived in Florida in the late Pleistocene. Modern bison survived in the state until they were extirpated around 1800, but a small wild herd was reintroduced in 1975 to Paynes Prairie State Preserve, south of Gainesville, and is growing in numbers. The end of the Pleistocene is known for the widespread extinctions of many vertebrates in North and South America, including twenty-four species of large mammals, two large birds, the giant tortoise, and several small mammals. The cause of the extinctions is unknown, although most scientists believe it may have been a combination of environmental changes and excessive predation by human hunters, who also immigrated to the New World at the end of the Pleistocene some ten thousand to fifteen thousand years ago.

Florida's Rain Barrels: The Floridan and Biscayne Aquifers

Much of Florida is covered by sand over a porous limestone substrate, a combination that does not allow rainwater to remain near the surface for long. Rain is essential for replenishing the relatively thin layer of surface water upon which most of Florida's ecosystems depend. Rainfall is also critical for recharging Florida's two major aquifers—the Floridan and Biscayne. The aquifers, underground layers of rock filled with groundwater, are formed as rainwater seeps down through porous soil and rock and accumulates above an impermeable rock formation.

The Floridan Aquifer is large and deep, extending from southern South Carolina across the lower half of Georgia and the southeastern corner of Alabama and underlying all of Florida. Because it traps so much water, it has been called Florida's rain barrel. Its principal recharge area, referred to in physi-

Late afternoon sunlight and dogwood flowers brighten a temperate hardwood hammock in Torreya State Park, along the bluffs of the Apalachicola River in the Panhandle.

Right: *Fossil coral makes up much of the Key Largo Limestone that is the upper layer of bedrock underlying much of the Florida Keys. This coral formation was found in the wall of a solution hole on Lignumvitae Key, Lignumvitae State Botanical Site.*
Below: *A prescribed fire burns through a freshwater marsh and cypress dome in Big Cypress National Preserve. Fire is critical for the survival of many upland ecosystems in Florida—particularly marshes, pinelands, and scrub—because it maintains an open, sun-drenched landscape needed by a wide variety of plants and animals. Historically, fires were started by lightning from late spring and early summer thunderstorms. About twelve thousand years ago, early Native Americans arrived in Florida and used fire to clear land for cultivation, flush game animals from heavy cover, and communicate with each other. Most fires are now set by park biologists to reap the benefits fires provide, while at the same time protecting against the fires spreading into areas populated by humans.*

ographic lingo as the Central Lake District, is a narrow region that runs like a broad pucker along the center of the state from north Florida through central Florida, encompassing the Kissimmee chain of lakes at its southern end. The Central Lake District is comprised primarily of lakes, sandhill, and sandpine scrub communities through which rainwater rapidly drains into the uplifted limestone of the aquifer. Recharge areas for the Floridan Aquifer also exist in Georgia and Alabama. A drop of water percolating downward in a roughly southwest direction through this aquifer takes thousands of years to reach the sea.

Although the Biscayne Aquifer is smaller and shallower than the Floridan Aquifer, it is considered one of the most permeable aquifers in the world. It underlies much of southeast Florida and is actually perched above the Floridan Aquifer in this part of the state. Layers of Tamiami limestone provide an impervious bottom, or aquiclude, for the Biscayne Aquifer, while Miami, Anastasia, Key Largo, and Fort Thompson limestones comprise the aquifer's permeable top layers. Together, the Floridan and Biscayne Aquifers provide more than 90 percent of the state's water for drinking, irrigation, recreation, and waste disposal.

Fire: Sculptor of Florida's Flora

Fire has been a major sculptor of Florida's landscape for at least several million years. Entire communities of plants and animals have evolved strategies to survive fires historically ignited by lightning in the late spring and early summer. Some twelve thousand years ago, early Native Americans arrived in Florida and used fire to clear land for cultivation, flush game animals from heavy cover, and communicate with each other. Their use of fire influenced the mosaic of ecosystems in the state as well.

Many natural communities in Florida owe their existence either to the frequent occurrence of fire or to its long absence. For example, longleaf pine forests are considered a pyrogenic landscape, one dependent on fire to retain its diversity and vigor. In these forests, periodic fires prune encroaching hardwoods that would otherwise steal nutrients and light from pines and herbaceous plants. Fire burns off groundcover and the accumulation of needle litter and deadwood to provide open bare soil for longleaf seedlings and other plants adapted to dry conditions to germinate in the fall. It also recycles nutrients in the soil and synchronizes the reproductive activity of grasses and wildflowers.

Factors such as the time of year a fire occurs, the interval between fires, and how hot a fire burns have a dramatic effect on the diversity and abundance of plants and animals after a fire. Without fire, a pineland may eventually become a forest dominated by hardwoods, resulting in the elimination of a wide array of plants and animals that cannot survive in a dense, shaded forest community.

Fire, however, is devastating to hardwood communities such as bottomland forests, temperate hardwood hammocks, and tropical hardwood hammocks—ecosystems that may require more than one hundred years without fire to mature. Stability is the key word for these forests, which support plants and animals adapted to moist, shady conditions and mild fluctuations of temperature. Damage from catastrophic events, such as a fires or hurricanes, sets back the successional clock by downing mature trees and creating openings in the canopy. These openings, or "gaps," allow light to flood the forest floor. Extremes in temperature are then greater, and humidity decreases, altering the microclimate and creating conditions more favorable to plants and animals that dominated the forest when it was younger and more dynamic.

A Landscape to Discover

Florida has long been a destination for explorers and treasure seekers. Some, including the Spanish conquistadors, expected to find material riches and the source of eternal life. Needless to say, they were disappointed in Florida. Others, including early naturalists John and William Bartram, John James Audubon, and John Muir, came in search of a more tangible treasure—the rich variety of Florida's wilderness. They were at once enthralled and uncomfortable with the strangeness of the landscape and its inhabitants.

Botanist William Bartram explored much of Florida in the mid-1700s. In his account, *Travels of William Bartram*, published in 1791, he writes, "Our repose however was incomplete, from the stings of

Red-cockaded woodpeckers, normally white with black markings, are an endangered species restricted primarily to pine flatwoods with imbedded clusters of large, mature trees in which they excavate cavities. This female, photographed after she was banded in Big Cypress Swamp, is an extremely rare pale color variation that is white with tan markings. Only one other red-cockaded woodpecker, a male captured many years earlier in Georgia, has been found with this coloration. The birds are not albinos because of the dark eyes, beak, and feet; the Georgia male's "cockade," a bright red patch toward the back of the head that is usually seen only when the bird is excited, was also normal.

musquetoes, the roaring of crocodiles [alligators], and the continual noise and restlessness of the sea fowl, thousands of them having their roosting places very near us, particularly loons of various species, herons, pelicans, Spanish curlews, &c. all promiscuously lodging together, and in such incredible numbers, that the trees were entirely covered."

Almost one hundred and fifty years later, naturalist John Muir walked through Florida, recording his musings in *A Thousand Mile Walk to the Gulf*, published in 1916. He writes, "I am now in the hot gardens of the sun, where the palm meets the pine, longed and prayed for and often visited in dreams, and, though lonely to-night amid this multitude of strangers, strange plants, strange winds blowing gently, whispering, cooing, in a language I never learned . . . I thank the Lord with all my heart for his goodness in granting me admission to this magnificent realm."

Florida's wild remnants still awe visitors with their subtle, mysterious beauty, although there is much less wilderness than what greeted eighteenth- and nineteenth-century naturalists. Recently, essayist John Jerome visited scrub in central Florida and wrote, "It was perversely amusing to camp there, in solitary wilderness splendor on a sandy desert ridge, surrounded by threatened species of both plants and animals, within half a mile of U.S. 27—the major north-south highway past Disney World's western entrance."

A proximity to civilization marks many of the "bits of the old wild left around," but there are isolated expanses of protected land remaining as well, including much of Everglades National Park, wilderness areas within Apalachicola, Osceola, and Ocala National Forests, and the glassy backcountry waters of the Keys. The Florida state park system alone includes more than 110 unique areas throughout the state—ample space to savor the call of a barred owl in a remote reach of swamp or end the day facing west on a quiet Gulf beach to admire what John Muir described as "another of the fine sunsets in this land of flowers." Slow your pace to the pulse of crickets along the banks of a Florida river, and you will lose your heart to the wild.

Florida Caverns State Park

Falling Waters State Recreation Area

OSCEOLA NATIONAL FOREST

Suwannee River State Park

Amelia Island

Big Talbot Island State Park

Little Talbot Island State Park

Ochlockonee River

Torreya State Park

TALLAHASSEE

St. Johns River

JACKSONVILLE

PENSACOLA

Suwannee River

O'Leno State Park

GULF ISLANDS NATIONAL SEASHORE

Grayton Beach SRA

Ichetucknee Springs State Park

San Felasco Hammock State Preserve

Paynes Prairie State Preserve

St. Joseph Peninsula State Park

GAINESVILLE

Washington Oaks State Gardens

St. George Island State Park

OCALA NATIONAL FOREST

CANAVERAL NATIONAL SEASHORE

APALACHICOLA NATIONAL FOREST

Manatee Springs State Park

Cedar Key

MERRITT ISLAND NATIONAL WILDLIFE REFUGE

LOWER SUWANNEE NATIONAL WILDLIFE REFUGE

ORLANDO

Gulf of Mexico

Hillsborough River State Park

TAMPA

Lake Kissimmee State Park

Kissimmee River

Atlantic Ocean

Highlands Hammock State Park

Jonathan Dickinson State Park

Myakka River State Park

Lake Okeechobee

WEST PALM BEACH

Cayo Costa State Park

LOXAHATCHEE NATIONAL WILDLIFE REFUGE

BIG CYPRESS NATIONAL PRESERVE

Fakahatchee Strand State Preserve

Florida

EVERGLADES NATIONAL PARK

MIAMI

Ten Thousand Islands

Cape Sable

John Pennekamp Coral Reef State Park

Florida Bay

Dry Tortugas

Lignumvitae Key State Botanical Site

FLORIDA KEYS NATIONAL WILDLIFE REFUGES

KEY WEST

Florida Keys

Map: *Florida's major national parks and forests as well as state parks and preserves noted in this book.*

Left: *Cumulus clouds floating through an azure sky are reflected by high water in a freshwater marsh at Big Cypress National Preserve. Tropical weather systems during the summer can dump several inches of rain at a time, causing water to rise in marshes and swamps. Rising water often forces deer, panthers, and other upland animals onto the higher ground of hammocks, sometimes limiting their ability to find food.*

Chapter 2

Florida's Natural Communities

"Here in this happy land of Florida all is different . . . the plants keep neither day
book nor ledger, they go by no calendar. . . . They live in a lazy country, a land of
mañana; they take the risk of frost and northers coming to spoil their growth
and nip their blossoms. . . . I have never seen a time during my twenty-five years'

residence in South Florida when I could not in any
extended walk gather at least fifty species of wild
plants in bloom." So responded Charles Torrey
Simpson in *Out of Doors in Florida*, published in
1924, to a question often asked of him by visitors
to Florida: "Where are the wild flowers?" Simpson
loved the state's diverse flora and frequently took
long walks in search of wildflowers, particularly in
the flatwoods, a "forest of old pine trees looking as
if they had all sprung from a single crop of seed a
long time ago."

Facing page: *Swamp lilies at Big Cypress National Preserve thrust forth from the tawny expanse of a
freshwater marsh like clusters of stars.*
Above: *A Gulf Coast box turtle wanders among reindeer moss lichens in a coastal scrub at St. Joseph
Peninsula State Park. This subspecies is the largest of the box turtles in Florida. In some areas, old males
may have white or cream-colored heads, such as the individual shown here.*

Other naturalists have been stirred by the spectacle of Florida's vegetation as well. John James Audubon described in his journals his first impression of Indian Key during his 1826 voyage to the St. Johns River and the Florida Keys: "With what delightful feelings did we gaze on the objects around us!—the gorgeous flowers, the singular and beautiful plants, the luxuriant trees."

Although there is little disagreement among naturalists over the aesthetic qualities of Florida's natural environment, there has always been considerable debate on how to classify its ecosystems. An ecosystem is a community of organisms and their environment interacting as an ecological unit. But classification is a subjective exercise that varies among scientists in different fields and, according to John J. Ewel, co-editor with Ronald L. Myers of *Ecosystems of Florida*, is largely dependent on a combination of floristics, physiognomy, environmental factors, and successional status. Various classifications during this century have set the number of ecosystems in the state at as few as ten to as many as eighty-one. As research reveals more about relationships among Florida's plants, animals, soil, hydrology, and other environmental factors, the existing classifications could change, possibly resulting in even more categories being established.

Scrub

Scrub is among the oldest of Florida's ecosystems, and possibly the driest. Many thousands of years ago, a wide belt of arid scrublands stretched from what is now the western United States east to the Atlantic Ocean, dipping south through northern Mexico and the southern United States. Glacial fluctuations, however, influenced climatic changes that essentially severed this belt, eliminating the eastern scrublands except for a few remnant patches scat-

A southern fence swift is remarkably camouflaged when pressed flat against a turkey oak in a sandhill community. The lizard sports splashes of yellow near its tail that mimic the yellow lichens growing on the oak, while its gray body color dappled with dark and light blotches matches the play of shadow and light on the rough bark.

tered on ancient sand dunes located primarily in central Florida. Cut off from western scrublands and shaped by Florida's seasonally wet, warm climate, Florida scrub evolved into an ecosystem unlike any other in the world.

Many scrubs in central Florida harbor dozens of plants and animals that are found nowhere else on earth, although some species have distant cousins in Mexico and the western United States. This strange and wonderful environment exists literally as a series of desertlike islands among the swamps, marshes, and soggy pine flatwoods that cover much of the state. Although scrub receives as much rain as other areas, its deep, well-drained sand allows water to pass through rapidly, forcing plants to evolve physiological strategies for efficiently gathering and retaining moisture. Scrub plants and animals have also evolved to survive the intense, although relatively infrequent fires that play a major role in keeping scrub vibrant and diverse.

According to Ronald L. Myers in *Ecosystems of Florida*, there are three major groupings of scrub: inland peninsula, coastal peninsula, and coastal Panhandle. Although the vegetation in these scrubs frequently differs from place to place, most scrubs look similar because they host the same dominant woody plants, such as sand pine, rosemary, and several species of dwarfed, gnarled evergreen scrub oaks.

Inland peninsula scrubs are concentrated along a series of sand ridges and ancient dunes running north to south from Clay and Putnam Counties in north Florida to Highlands County in central Florida. These ridges make up the Florida Central Ridge and formed during the Miocene through the early Pleistocene Epochs over the course of several million years. The highest crests of the Florida Central Ridge are of Miocene origin and were once islands when much of Florida was covered by a shallow sea. The inland peninsula scrubs are the largest remaining areas of scrub, and those on the Lake Wales Ridge are home to the highest number of endemic species.

Coastal peninsula scrubs are found on both the Atlantic and Gulf coasts of peninsular Florida. They are associated with ancient dunes that bordered the Pamlico and Silver Bluff shorelines of the late Pleistocene. The northernmost coastal peninsula scrubs are in St. Johns County on the east coast and in Levy County near Cedar Key on the Gulf Coast. Elsewhere, you can find coastal peninsula scrubs at Merritt Island National Wildlife Refuge near Cape Canaveral, and at Jonathan Dickinson State Park and Hobe Sound National Wildlife Refuge in southeast Florida. On the west coast, the southernmost scrub is at Rookery Bay Reserve, just north of Marco Island.

Coastal Panhandle scrubs are limited to a narrow strip of shoreline and barrier islands along the Panhandle Gulf Coast, stretching west from the Ochlockonee River to Gulf Bay State Park in Alabama. They too are perched on old dunes from the Pamlico and Silver Bluff shorelines, as well as on stable dunes that may have formed within the last one hundred years.

Sandhill and Clayhill

Rolling hills of deep sand covered by forests of widely spaced pines and deciduous oaks occur in many areas of Florida, particularly in the Panhandle and northern half of the state. A seasonally dense groundcover of grasses and wildflowers spreads like a flowing, multi-hued blanket beneath the trees. These are sandhill and clayhill communities, which like scrub and other ecosystems dominated by a pine canopy, are pyrogenic, or dependent on fire to thrive. Longleaf pine is the primary canopy species, although slash pine replaces longleaf in south Florida. Turkey oak dominates the understory trees, and wiregrass is the principal grass. Longleaf pine and wiregrass provide the primary fuel for fire in sandhills and clayhills, and both species need fire to reproduce. Other common plants found in sandhill and clayhill ecosystems are bluejack oak, sand post oak, runner oak, sparkleberry, persimmon, winged

sumac, pinewoods dropseed, Indian grass, wild buckwheat, partridge pea, gopher apple, golden aster, blue twinflower, and blazing star.

The gopher tortoise and southern fence lizard are probably the two most prevalent reptiles you'll see on a hike through sandhill or clayhill, but you might also find an indigo snake, coachwhip snake, crowned snake, eastern diamondback rattlesnake, or a mole skink. In spite of the dryness of sandhills, there are still amphibians, including the tiger salamander, barking tree frog, spadefoot toad, and gopher frog. These creatures lay their eggs in ephemeral sandhill ponds without fish. Bobwhite, rufous-sided towhees, ground doves, and red-shouldered hawks are common.

In appearance, sandhill and clayhill communities are quite similar, except that clayhill vegetation is somewhat more luxuriant because of the relatively moist, fertile, clay-rich soil. Sandhill communities occur on dry, infertile, coarse sand indicative of Pleistocene sand ridges. Outside of Florida, similar ecosystems extend up the coastal plain to the Carolinas and Virginia and westward into Alabama, Mississippi, and east Texas. The end of the sand ridges in peninsular Florida marks the southern limits of sandhill, reaching down to Martin County on the east coast, Lee County on the west coast, and Highlands County in the interior.

Native Dry Prairies

Among the most characteristic features of south-central Florida are its dry prairies—open grasslands with scattered saw palmettos and oak/cabbage palm hammocks—that occur north and west of Lake Okeechobee along the Kissimmee River, as well as farther west in Desoto and Sarasota Counties. Unfortunately, most native dry prairies have been converted to ranch land, so only small patches of what was once an extensive landscape survives. What remains is important habitat for animals that occur nowhere else in the eastern United States, such as the threatened crested caracara and burrowing owl.

Native dry prairies occupy flat, poorly drained terrain that may occasionally flood for short periods during the rainy season. They too depend on fires every one to four years to maintain a grassy landscape with few trees. Common plants of native

Right, top: *The morning sun punches through building thunderheads over the National Audubon Society's Ordway-Whittel Kissimmee Prairie Preserve in central Florida. Native dry prairie is an ecosystem unique to Florida.*

Right, bottom: *Storm clouds build over an island of pine rocklands surrounded by saw grass marsh in Everglades National Park.*

dry prairies include broomsedge, carpet grass, wiregrass, Indian grass, love grass, saw palmetto, blazing star, rabbit tobacco, pine lily, marsh pink, milkwort, goldenrod, pawpaw, gallberry, stagger bush, fetterbush, and dwarf blueberry. Numerous carnivorous plants are found here as well, which is indicative of the nutrient-poor nature of the habitat. These carnivorous plants include sundews, butterworts, and various species of pitcher plants.

Wildlife living on dry prairies includes the Florida box turtle, six-lined race-runner, coachwhip snake, black racer, Florida sandhill crane, turkey and black vultures, meadowlark, ground dove, mottled duck, loggerhead shrike, grasshopper sparrow, least shrew, cotton rat, harvest mouse, Florida water rat, spotted skunk, and bobcat.

Pine Flatwoods

According to the Florida Natural Areas Inventory, pine flatwoods are the most widespread natural community in Florida, occupying an estimated 30 to 50 percent of the state's uplands. Pine flatwoods are topographically flat; rooted in poorly drained, acidic, sandy soil; and experience relatively frequent fires. They range in appearance from open forests of scattered pines with little understory to dense pine stands with a thick undergrowth of grasses, saw palmettos, and low shrubs. Longleaf pine, slash pine,

pond pine, and south Florida slash pine (a more fire-tolerant, drought-resistant south Florida variety of the slash pine) dominate the canopy in either pure or mixed stands. Typical understory shrubs include saw palmetto, gallberry, fetterbush, staggerbush, dwarf huckleberry, wax myrtle, dwarf live oak, and tarflower.

Because pines drop their lower branches, they leave a large gap between the canopy and the layer of shrubs below. A diverse, fecund groundcover of herbaceous wildflowers and grasses, especially wiregrass, the most characteristic grass in flatwoods, appears only in stands of pine with a relatively open canopy and shrub understory—the result of frequent fires.

Flatwoods habitat supports a diverse population of birds; small mammals such as the cotton rat, cotton mouse, and short-tailed shrew; twenty to thirty species of reptiles and amphibians; and a few large mammals, including whitetailed deer, black bear, and Florida panther.

Pine flatwoods occur throughout the state and as a result, the climate of these forests varies from warm temperate in the northern portion of the state to subtropical in south Florida. Geographic location and climate, the seasonal cycle of flood and drought and its impact on soil and hydrology, fire frequency, and degradation due to human activities profoundly influence the diversity and composition of plants in pine flatwoods, and to a more limited degree, wildlife. For example, wet flatwoods occur in low areas that are frequently flooded, and they may contain standing water for one or two months every year. In north and central Florida, the canopy of these forests generally consists of slash pine, pond pine, and cabbage palm. Pond pine does not grow farther south than central Florida, and south Florida flatwoods are typically dominated by south Florida slash pine and cabbage palm in the canopy. Water-tolerant shrubs such as wax myrtle and gallberry fill in the understory. Mesic flatwoods, on the other hand, occur on somewhat higher, drier locations and are seldom inundated. They are dominated by a canopy of slash or longleaf pine and a dense understory of saw palmetto. Gallberry, rusty lyonia, wax myrtle, and wiregrass are common. There is considerable overlap in the species of understory shrubs among pine flatwoods. Saw palmetto and gallberry monopolize the shrub layer in slash pine flatwoods; wiregrass and running oak reign in longleaf pine flatwoods; and fetterbush and several species of bay trees hold sway in the soggy pond pine areas.

In north and central Florida, longleaf pine is the typical pine of the better-drained flatwoods, slash pine rules swamps and the perimeter of ponds, and pond pine predominates in poorly drained flatwoods. Other trees that may occur in north and central Florida flatwoods include live oak, water oak, sweet gum, red maple, and ash. In south Florida, the only flatwoods pine is south Florida slash pine. Throughout Florida, large areas of pine flatwoods form an extensive matrix intermixed with seasonal ponds, bay heads, cypress heads and ponds, bogs, titi swamps, cabbage palm hammocks, temperate hardwood hammocks, sandhill, or scrub.

Unfortunately, few stands of pine flatwoods today reflect conditions as they were before the arrival of Europeans to Florida. Agriculture, livestock grazing, tree farming, fire suppression, and urban development have exacted a heavy toll, and most present-day stands differ from those of presettlement days by having

Basket oaks and other hardwoods seem to glow under a canopy of new spring growth at San Felasco Hammock State Preserve in north Florida. Florida has no vast forests of hardwoods. Instead, they occur as hammocks, or islands of hardwoods, that form narrow forested bands on slopes between sandhill or clayhill pinelands and bottomland habitat, such as lake margins or floodplain forests.

31

The tannin-stained waters of the Hillsborough River flow around bald cypress and an island of water oaks and other hardwoods at Hillsborough River State Park, just north of Tampa. Florida's rivers are among its most precious treasures.

lower fire frequencies, a more even age structure, and a denser understory with more shrubs and fewer grasses and wildflowers.

Pine Rocklands

Pine rocklands are limited to an area of south Florida stretching from the southern Everglades west to eastern Big Cypress Swamp. They are also found on several islands in the lower Keys. This natural community is characterized by an open canopy of south Florida slash pine growing on raised outcrops of oolitic limestone. Beneath the canopy struggles a scattered understory of tropical and temperate shrubs and palms, as well as a sparse groundcover of grasses and herbaceous wildflowers.

Pine rockland forests in south Florida develop on locally elevated areas of limestone bedrock bordered primarily by wet prairies, and in the lower Florida Keys, by mangroves. Only a thin layer of soil covers the bare limestone, although it sometimes accumulates in holes and crevices in the rock. As with pine flatwoods in other parts of the state, the elevation of these pine forests varies from a few inches above surrounding marshy areas to a few feet.

Pine rocklands harbor a diverse array of tropical and subtropical plants and animals, several of which are considered endangered, threatened, or rare. Some of these species are common in the West Indies, but have either strayed or reach the extreme northern limit of their range in the pine rocklands. Many are endemic, including five spurges, sand flax, queen's delight, pineland jacquemontia, Big Pine partridge pea, and pineland noseburn. Common pine rockland plants include saw palmetto, cabbage palm, silver palm, gallberry, velvet seed, blolly, poisonwood, bustic, live oak, stoppers, shining sumac, satin leaf, wild tamarind, rubber vine, snowberry, broomsedge, wiregrass, muhly grass, partridge pea, coontie, and pinefern. Wildlife includes the southeastern five-lined skink, ringneck snake, pygmy

33

Fern Hammock Spring is but one of several springs in the Ocala National Forest in central Florida. Florida has more than three hundred springs, which range from cool, freshwater seeps to warm mineral springs.

rattlesnake, red-shouldered hawk, Carolina wren, eastern bluebird, pine warbler, opossum, marsh rabbit, cotton rat, cotton mouse, raccoon, and bobcat. The Key deer is endemic to pine rocklands in the lower Keys.

Temperate Hardwood Hammocks

Florida has no vast forests of hardwoods. Instead, they occur as hammocks, or islands of hardwoods, that form narrow forested bands on slopes between sandhill or clayhill pinelands and bottomland habitat such as lake margins or floodplain forests. Temperate hardwood hammocks are found throughout most of Florida, but the plants in these forests vary from warm temperate species in the north to tropical species in the south. The temperate hardwood

hammocks in the northern part of Florida are said to have the highest number of species of trees and shrubs found together anywhere in the continental United States. These hammocks support a diverse blend of deciduous and broad-leaved evergreen trees and shrubs, although the number of evergreen plants increases as diversity decreases in central and south Florida.

Peninsular hammocks situated around sinkholes also contain myriad tropical and temperate ferns. This is because the sinkholes create a habitat that is cooler in the summer due to the shade offered in their depths and warmer in the winter because of constant water flow.

The largest, most diverse hammocks are located in the Panhandle and include white oak, southern

Hardwoods surrounding a sinkhole at Paynes Prairie State Preserve in northern Florida seem to bend gently toward the gossamer light of a foggy, autumn morning.

beech, southern magnolia, sweetgum, American holly, Florida maple, spruce pine, and live oak as common species. In north and central Florida, the hammocks that cloak the central ridge of the peninsula are similar to those of the Panhandle except that they lack white oak and southern beech. Hammocks located on the Atlantic and Gulf coasts, often called maritime hammocks, as well as hammocks on the southern end of the central Florida ridge, contain mainly tropical or broad-leaved evergreen overstory trees. Live oak, cabbage palm, southern magnolia, redbay, strangler fig, and ironwood are among the most common trees in these hammocks. Tropical shrubs dominate the understory, while Spanish moss, an epiphytic bromeliad related to pineapple, hangs from the trees.

Whitetailed deer and gray squirrels are the most noticeable mammals during the day. Southern flying squirrels, opossums, raccoons, and armadillos come out at night. Red-shouldered hawks, barred owls, pileated woodpeckers, and a wide variety of warblers are among the most striking and common birds.

Tropical Hardwood Hammocks

Tropical hardwood hammocks are found only in extreme south Florida and in the Keys. They are considered among the rarest ecosystems in North America because of development pressure from urban expansion.

Like pine rocklands, tropical hardwood hammocks occur on outcrops of exposed or nearly exposed limestone in thin, rich soil, and in the absence of fire, a pine rockland may transform into a tropical hardwood hammock. In the Everglades and lower Keys, tropical hardwood hammocks are often surrounded by pine forest. Tropical trees are predominant in these hammocks and include gumbo limbo, wild tamarind, pigeon plum, poisonwood, mahogany, strangler fig, Jamaica dogwood, lignum vitae, and several species of stoppers. Tropical shrubs, such as wild coffee, white indigoberry, and satinleaf, form a diverse understory, and orchids and bromeliads festoon the branches of many trees.

Rare and beautiful creatures such as Schaus' swallowtail, *Liguus* treesnails, and white-crowned pigeons are found in these hammocks, as well as woodrats including the endangered Key Largo woodrat, cottonmice, raccoons, opossums, and several species of reptiles.

Freshwater Swamps and Floodplain Forests

Anyone who visits Florida expects to see swamp, and the diversity of swamps in the state is remarkable. Heads, domes, strands, bogs, and galls are only a few of the different varieties of swamp distributed throughout the state. Many swamps in Florida are comprised of a matrix of natural communities, including uplands, hydric hammocks, poorly drained pine flatwoods, shrub bogs, and cypress wetlands. Some of these landscapes cover large areas, such as Tate's Hell in the Panhandle, Osceola National Forest in northeast Florida, Gulf Hammock near Cedar Key on the Gulf Coast, the Green Swamp in central Florida, and Big Cypress Swamp in south Florida.

The blending of temperate and tropical species makes Florida swamps unique among North American wetlands. Some of these swamps are among the last places in Florida to find black bear and panther.

Floodplain forests, considered by many ecologists to be a type of river swamp, occur primarily in the northern half of Florida along rivers. They have a distinct hydroperiod, or length of time during the year in which they are flooded, but it is typically shorter than in other swamps. Classic examples of floodplain forest grow along the Apalachicola River, Suwannee River, and Oklawaha River.

Freshwater Marshes and Wet Prairies

Freshwater marshes are wetlands dominated by emergent, herbaceous plants inundated by shallow water for much of the year. Marshes differ from swamps in that less than one-third of marsh vegetation consists of trees and shrubs. They are classified according to their physiognomy (characteristic features or appearance of their vegetation), such as floodplain marsh, swale marsh, or depression marsh, and by the dominant plants in the community, such as saw grass marsh or flag marsh.

Wet prairies are similar to freshwater marshes, except that they have much shorter hydroperiods, thereby allowing many plants unable to tolerate the extended wet periods of marshes to thrive. Frequent fires are critical to both ecosystems to prevent hardwood shrubs from taking over and to maintain the diversity of herbaceous plants.

Common plants in freshwater marshes and wet prairies include several species of grasses and sedges, such as maidencane, toothache grass, spikerush, beakrush, muhly grass, and saw grass, as well as pickerelweed, arrowheads, many species of wildflowers, and a few shrubs. Few large mammals spend much time in these soggy ecosystems, although swamp rabbits, cotton rats, and cotton mice are prevalent.

Florida is renowned for its freshwater marshes, especially the saw grass expanse of the Everglades in southern Florida. Other large marshes include Paynes Prairie in north-central Florida, the marshes surrounding Lake Okeechobee, and the floodplain marshes along the Kissimmee and St. Johns Rivers. Few freshwater marshes are found in the Panhandle or along the central ridge of the state because the land is elevated and rainwater runs off quickly. The rest of the state is low-lying, poorly drained, and flat. In the case of the Everglades, rainwater is impounded by the limestone and sand of coastal ridges and topographic rises, much like soup is contained within a bowl. In other parts of the state, freshwater marshes occur in shallow depressions or along lakes and rivers, where water cannot drain away quickly.

Pitcher Plant Bogs

Pitcher plant bogs are known by many names, including herb bogs, seepage bogs, river terrace bogs, or savanna bogs. These fascinating, fire-dependent

pine barrens tree frog, squirrel tree frog, ribbon snake, and cottonmouth are common. Several endemic plants are found in the pine flatwoods and pitcher plant bogs of the Apalachicola National Forest, including violet-flowered butterwort, tropical waxweed, Harper's beauty, Panhandle spider lily, thick-leaved water willow, white birds-in-a-nest, Curtiss' loosestrife, giant water dropwort, dark-headed hatpins, Apalachicola dragonhead, Florida skullcap, and pineland false sunflower. Blackwater River State Forest and Eglin Air Force Base in the Panhandle, as well as a few bogs in the Osceola National Forest in northeast Florida, also contain a tremendous diversity of creatures and plants.

wetlands are found in the Florida Panhandle, southern Alabama, and southern Mississippi, in association with large stands of longleaf pine, areas of mixed pines and hardwoods, and strips of live oak near the coast. Pitcher plant bogs develop on acidic, water-saturated, nutrient-poor, sandy soil that rarely floods. The soil lies on top of an impermeable layer of rock or clay that prevents water from draining.

Carnivorous plants such as sundews, bladderworts, butterworts, and pitcher plants thrive beneath an open canopy of pond pine, slash pine, or longleaf pine. Bog-loving shrubs found in these natural communities include titi, fetterbush, gallberry, dahoon holly, wax myrtle, and Virginia willow. The colorful

Lakes and Ponds

There are few large lakes in Florida, but thousands of small ones. Lake Okeechobee, Lake George, Lake Kissimmee, Lake Apopka, and Lake Istokpoga are the only lakes with surface areas greater than sixty-two square miles. Most Florida lakes are warm, clear, nutrient-poor, and shallow. Three-quarters of them, including Lake Okeechobee, are no deeper than seventeen feet. A few lakes, however, are deeper than eighty feet, such as Deep Lake in Big Cypress Swamp, which is more than ninety-five feet deep.

The vast majority of Florida lakes are concentrated in central Florida, creating a lake district unique in the southern United States. Most Florida lakes are seepage lakes, meaning that much of the water flowing in is groundwater. More than 70 percent of these lakes lack an outward drainage, such as a river or stream. Lakes in Florida take on many forms, occurring as shallow freshwater depressions behind dune systems near the coast; as ephemeral ponds in sandhills, prairies, and flatwoods; as shallow, open water areas within swamps; and as deep, water-filled, funnel-shaped depressions in the limestone. Vegetation rimming these lakes and ponds may consist of broad bands of hydrophytic (water-loving) grasses and other herbaceous species, dense thickets of shrubs, or narrow bands of grasses and wildflowers similar to those in wet prairies. Even the Keys have ponds—small depressions in the limestone filled with water from underlying fresh groundwater lenses floating on top of denser, saltier groundwater.

Wherever lakes and ponds occur, they are important sources of drinking water for animals and birds; breeding grounds for amphibians; and home for freshwater fish, including largemouth bass, bluegill and other panfish, redfin pickerel, alligator gar, and a host of minnows. Alligators and turtles, of course, are residents as well.

Rivers

Most of Florida's more than 1,700 rivers originate within the state and flow toward the Gulf of Mexico. The St. Johns, St. Marys, and Loxahatchee Rivers are among the few that drain into the Atlantic. The St. Johns is the longest river completely within Florida, originating in the Kissimmee Prairie and flowing north for a distance of some 317 miles until it meets the Atlantic Ocean just north of Jacksonville. The Suwannee is the second longest river in Florida, although its headwaters are in Georgia's Okefenokee Swamp. The Apalachicola River is probably the grandest river overall, with the broadest drainage basin (32,116 square miles), the greatest average discharge, and longest total length (498 miles), although only a small portion of the whole system is

within Florida. Historically, the Flint and the Chattahoochee Rivers flowed south from Alabama and Georgia to form the Apalachicola, but the area of confluence was impounded by the construction of the Jim Woodruff Dam, creating Lake Seminole, now the headwaters of the Apalachicola. The Kissimmee River, which flows south through the Osceola Plain on its way to Lake Okeechobee in south Florida, is the only major river that does not drain directly into either the Atlantic or the Gulf of Mexico.

There are several varieties of rivers in Florida. Probably the most abundant type is the sand-bottomed, or blackwater, rivers, found primarily in the Panhandle and upper Gulf Coast. The term "blackwater" derives from the dark, tea-colored water, stained by tannin from decaying leaves and dissolved organic matter as it runs through swamps and marshes. Submerged, aquatic vegetation is rare because the dark water reduces the amount of light that penetrates below the surface, inhibiting photosynthesis. The current is moderate to fast, creating ideal conditions for a variety of immature insects adapted to swift water, including mayflies, caddisflies, and blackflies. Water temperature may fluctuate with air temperature. These rivers typically have high, steep banks and lack the continuous, broad floodplain or natural levees created by other riverine systems.

Florida's famous spring-run, or calcareous, rivers are found predominately in the northern half of the state and originate from springs bubbling up from the Floridan Aquifer. Because the water emanates from underground and has been filtered by sand and limestone, it is relatively clear and cool throughout the year, allowing dense growths of several species of submerged, aquatic vegetation to thrive on the river bottom. The plants in turn provide shelter and food for an extensive web of life in the river. Mollusks are abundant in these rivers, possibly because of the water's high calcium content. This river type also includes subterranean rivers, which are common in the Floridan Aquifer, often flowing through large caverns. Part of the Santa Fe River in north Florida is subterranean; it disappears into a sinkhole in O'Leno State Park and emerges nearly two miles away at River Rise State Preserve.

Alluvial rivers are rare in Florida and are generally restricted to the northern Panhandle. They are characterized by extremely variable flow rates, high turbidity, and a considerable difference in water depth between normal and flood stages. Flood stages are important for these river systems because they transport detritus, minerals, and nutrients from upland areas to the lower-lying floodplain communities. Floodstage waters carry nutrients downstream to estuarine systems at the mouth of a river, expand the feeding range and habitat of fish and other aquatic creatures normally restricted to the main stream, and transport seeds and small animals to distant areas they could not otherwise reach. The rise and subsequent drop of flood waters also may stimulate the breeding cycles of many aquatic and semi-aquatic organisms and induce the hatching of eggs or development of larvae in others. Few rooted, aquatic plants can grow in turbid alluvial rivers for the same reasons as in blackwater rivers—light cannot penetrate to the river bottom, preventing photosynthesis in plants. The Apalachicola River is Florida's best known alluvial river.

Other types of river habitat in Florida include swamp-and-bog streams and seepage streams. Swamp-and-bog rivers and streams, as their name implies, originate from swamps, bogs, and marshes. They are generally acidic, deeply colored, and sluggish. Few invertebrates can survive in these rivers, but they host many species of fish.

Seepage streams originate from shallow groundwater that has percolated through deep sandy upland soil. The water is clear and cool and flows slowly, sometimes allowing leaf litter to collect near bends in the stream. Little vegetation generally grows in or around these streams because they are often shaded by a dense canopy of broad-leaved hardwoods. Seepage streams occur in hilly areas of north Florida and the Panhandle.

Some rivers do not fit within a single classification because there may be several sources of water flowing into them along their course. For example, the Aucilla River, which drains into Apalachee Bay on the northern Gulf coast, actually begins as a spring-run river, but becomes brown and acidic when it receives discharge from swamps and surface runoff below its headwaters. The Suwannee and Wacassassa Rivers emerge from swamps as acidic, dark streams, but receive an influx of clear, cool water from springs along their midsections.

The Famous Florida Springs

Florida is famous for its more than three hundred springs, which range from cool freshwater seeps to warm mineral springs. Most of Florida's springs are artesian and vary considerably in salinity, mineral content, and chemical features, including pH. The temperature of springs in the northern half of the state ranges from 66-75° Fahrenheit, while water temperature in springs farther south ranges from 75-87° F. Florida's warm climate, abundant rainfall, high humidity, tremendous quantity of decaying vegetation, and thick limestone bedrock make the state among the most favorable regions in the world for the formation of springs.

The magnitude of a spring is measured by the volume of water it produces over a given amount of time, expressed in the number of cubic feet per second or millions of gallons per day (mgd). Twenty-seven springs in Florida are first magnitude springs with average flow rates of at least 100 ft^3/sec or 64.6 mgd; these springs comprise approximately one-third of all first-magnitude springs in the United States. These twenty-seven springs produce a combined flow rate of six billion gallons per day.

Florida's remaining springs are second and third magnitude. There are about seventy second-magnitude springs with average flow rates between 10 and 100 ft^3/sec or 6.46 and 64.6 mgd. There are also approximately 190 third-magnitude springs with average flow rates less than 10 ft^3/sec. or 6.46 mgd. Together they produce only about one-fourth of the spring flow in the state.

Silver, Ichetucknee, Wakulla, and Homosassa Springs are among the most beautiful and best known in the state. The majority of Florida's springs are located in north and central Florida, although a few are found in the Panhandle and in south Florida.

Sinkholes

Sinkholes are a prominent feature of the karst terrain that covers much of the northern half of Florida. The limestone of this area is riddled with caverns created by the physical and chemical action of un-

Above: *A live oak at the edge of a salt marsh is warmed by the late afternoon sun on what had been a clear, bitterly cold day at Big Talbot Island State Park, just north of Jacksonville. Salt marshes thrive in low-lying intertidal areas along the coast where wave action is minimal and mangroves are either scattered or nonexistent. The salt marshes of northeast Florida are flooded twice a day by the highest tides in the state.*
Right: *An outgoing tide swirls past the exposed roots of red mangroves on a mud flat in the Keys near sunset, Great White Heron National Wildlife Refuge.*

derground water. A sinkhole is formed when the water table drops and hydrostatic pressure within an underwater cavern can no longer support the cavern's roof, causing it to collapse and bring with it loose sand and soil that had covered the top layer of limestone. A sinkhole is typically circular in shape, with steep limestone walls. If debris that fell into the cavity does not completely block the sinkhole's connection to the water table, the sinkhole may act as an aquifer recharge area. Many sinkholes are at least partially filled with water through much of the year, especially when the underlying aquifer is full. Many natural lakes in Florida are the result of sinkholes.

Sinkholes are often surrounded by an upland hardwood forest and provide refuge for many species of plants and animals that cannot survive elsewhere in the forest. The interior of a sinkhole is characterized by a moist microclimate, formed in part by the high humidity from standing water at the

bottom of the depression and seepage from the surrounding forest trickling down its sides. Wind cannot enter the sinkhole, and the dense canopy of hardwoods offers almost constant shade. The sinkhole provides the immediate area of surrounding forest with a fire shadow, so named because the damp conditions around the sinkhole can block the advance of a fire.

Caves

Many people are surprised to learn that Florida has an extensive system of caverns. Most caverns are filled with water, but there are two major clusters of air-filled caves. The first is in Jackson County in the Panhandle, near the town of Marianna, while the other straddles north and central Florida in a region encompassing Alachua, Marion, and Citrus Counties. Air-filled caves in Florida are relatively small and usually represent the upper parts of water-filled caverns.

Beaches, Dunes, and Barrier Islands

Florida's beaches are probably its greatest natural tourist attraction. They are also among its most beautiful and threatened natural communities.

Nearly 750 miles of the Florida coastline is sand, primarily in the form of offshore barrier islands. Dunes develop on these islands on both the Atlantic and Gulf coasts; behind these dunes, maritime forests grow. The only long stretches of coast without much sand are the mangrove swamps at the state's southern tip and in the Keys, as well as the expanses of salt marsh in the Big Bend region of the Gulf Coast, where the peninsula curves west to meet the Panhandle.

Beaches in Florida are composed primarily of quartz sand in the northern half of the state and quartz mixed with calcium carbonate sand from shell fragments and oolitic grains in the south. Barrier islands fringing the Panhandle are 99 percent quartz sand, which often squeaks like snow when you walk on it.

The quartz sand originated in the prehistoric Appalachians and tumbled down to Florida with rivers draining the Piedmont, including the Apalachicola and Ochlockonee Rivers in the Panhandle and the Santee, Savannah, and Altamaha Rivers in Georgia and South Carolina. As the sea level rose and fell across the continental shelf during the Pleistocene, these quartz sands were distributed along the coast by waves to form beaches and barrier islands. Longshore currents move the sand south along the Atlantic coast to about Cape Florida, south of Miami. In the Panhandle west of Cape San Blas, currents move sand westward. East of Cape San Blas, longshore drift moves sand both east and west.

Quartz sand beaches are also found on the Gulf Coast from Cape Romano north to the Anclote Keys, where like the southern barrier islands along the Atlantic Coast, they contain a high percentage of shell. Longshore currents in this region typically carry sand north from Indian Rocks Beach near Tampa Bay; south of Indian Rocks Beach, sand moves both north and south. Calcium carbonate sand (from pulverized seashells) forms the beaches of the Keys, Cape Sable, and the Ten Thousand Islands.

According to Ann Johnson and Michael Barbour in their chapter on dunes and maritime forests in *Ecosystems of Florida*, "The Florida coast can be divided into five regions, the beaches within each region having roughly similar vegetation: the northeast coast from the Georgia border to Cape Canaveral; the southeast coast from Cape Canaveral to Cape Florida; the south coast comprising the 'shell hash' and calcium carbonate sand beaches of Cape Sable, the Ten Thousand Islands, and the Florida Keys; the southwest coast from Cape Romano to Anclote Keys north of Tampa; and the Panhandle from the mouth of the Ochlockonee River west to the Alabama border."

Among regions, however, vegetation behind the dunes varies dramatically. For example, if you hike on the northeastern tip of Amelia Island, you will enjoy the deep shade of large live oaks and magnolias. A stroll behind the dunes along one of the rare undeveloped stretches of barrier island in Palm Beach County will take you through a lower, but more diverse subtropical forest of sea grape, stoppers, and gumbo limbo. If you visit Cayo Costa, which lies seaward of Fort Myers on the west coast, you will probably bake under the intense Florida sun in a shadeless cabbage palm savanna. On St. George Island in the Panhandle, you will encounter scrubby oaks and rosemary on the backdune, with slash pine flatwoods on the swale sloping down to Apalachicola Bay. Twenty-two plant species are thought to be found only along the Florida coast, including peninsular endemics such as the beach sunflower and beach verbena on the east coast and Florida yellowtop on the west coast.

Salt Marshes

Salt marshes thrive in low-lying intertidal areas along the coast where wave action is minimal and mangroves are either scattered or nonexistent. Black needlerush and smooth cordgrass dominate Florida's salt marshes, with glasswort, saltwort, salt grass, sea purslane, sea lavender, and other herbaceous, salt-tolerant plants abundant as well. When salt marshes flood, marine organisms move in, using the vegetation for food and cover. A network of tidal creeks allows larger creatures to escape before they are stranded by the low tide.

Salt marshes are concentrated in four parts of the state: Approximately 20 percent of the state's salt marshes occur in northeast Florida, 50 percent in northwest Florida, 10 percent in the Indian River Lagoon along the Atlantic coast, and the remaining 20 percent in south Florida. The composition of vegetation differs considerably among these salt marshes because of variations in tidal range and frequency, annual average temperature, and topography.

Salt marshes in northeast Florida, which extend from the Georgia border south to just below St. Augustine, are similar in vegetation, hydrology, and climate to Georgia's salt marshes. These salt marshes, distinguished by large expanses of smooth cordgrass, are flooded twice a day by the highest tides in Florida.

Salt marshes along the Gulf Coast extend from Tampa Bay to the Alabama border, especially in the Big Bend area (also known as the Nature Coast) from Aripeka to Apalachicola Bay. More than half of these salt marshes, which are similar to those in Alabama, Mississippi, and Louisiana, are dominated by monospecific stands of black needlerush that grow nearly to the water's edge. Salt marshes along the Gulf Coast are generally flooded only by extremely high tides, such as when a seasonal rise in sea level combines with high lunar and windblown tides. Historically, this was the same situation with salt marshes in the Indian River Lagoon, which are also above mean high tide. Unfortunately, nearly all of these salt marshes have been diked and are flooded for much of the year to control mosquitoes.

In areas of south Florida where mangrove swamps are well developed, salt marsh plants are restricted to the seaward and landward intertidal fringes. Smooth cordgrass grows in a narrow zone seaward of red mangroves, but the best-developed zones of salt marsh occur inland from the mangroves. These salt marshes are seldom inundated by salt water and vary in appearance from narrow strips to sprawling zones of black needlerush and other salt-tolerant plants. They are most extensive in Dade County south of Homestead and develop to a lesser extent from the southwest coast north to Tampa Bay. Inland, they may fade to barren salt pans or border vast expanses of saw grass.

Mangrove Swamps

Mangrove swamps in Florida are predominantly in the southern half of the state and limited to low-energy coastlines, meaning that they have little wave action. They vary tremendously in their structural appearance, ranging from tall, dense forests reaching heights of nearly seventy feet, such as along the Shark River in Everglades National Park, to dwarfed, scattered clumps on marl prairies in the southeastern Everglades. According to the Florida Natural Areas Inventory, they may develop as overwash swamps found on islands frequently flooded by tides; fringe swamps that border bays and waterways; riverine swamps found along tidal rivers and creeks; basin swamps that occupy low-lying areas inland from fringing and riverine swamps; hammock swamps, which are similar to basin swamps except that they command higher ground; and scrub swamps, which occur on limestone marl.

Four species of trees dominate mangrove swamps: red mangrove, black mangrove, white mangrove, and buttonwood. Other common plants include salt grass, black needlerush, spike rush, glasswort, Gulf cordgrass, sea purslane, saltwort, and sea oxeye. Mangrove swamps, in conjunction with other estuarine areas, are considered nursery grounds for many

reef fish, as well as for virtually all fish and shellfish valued by commercial and recreational fishermen.

Both red and white mangroves are reported as far north as Cedar Key on the west coast and north of Cape Canaveral on the east coast. They begin to grow thicker and taller south of Cape Canaveral on the east coast and Tarpon Springs on the west coast. Black mangroves are found as far north as St. Augustine on the east coast and occur as scattered shrubs along the north coast of the Gulf of Mexico. Approximately 90 percent of Florida's mangrove swamps are found at the state's southern tip and in the Keys.

Bays and Estuaries

Bays and estuaries occur along the Florida coast where fresh water mixes with the Gulf of Mexico and the Atlantic Ocean. In the northern half of the state, extensive salt marshes rim these broad, shallow bodies of water, while mangrove swamps thrive in similar areas to the south. Hard bottom and soft bottom habitats, sea grass beds, and oyster bars are found in estuaries and bays on both coasts, as are salt marshes and mangrove swamps. More than 90 percent of the species sought by sport and commercial fisheries use inshore habitats during some part of their life cycle.

Florida's east coast, from the mouth of the St. Johns River near Jacksonville to Biscayne Bay near Miami, is a high-energy shoreline (one with constant wave action) of barrier islands and lagoons. The lagoons lie between the barrier islands and the mainland. Coral reefs, lagoons, and Florida Bay comprise the nearshore environment south of Biscayne Bay.

Sunset glows over Apalachicola Bay, St. George Island State Park. Estuaries and bays occur along the Florida coast where fresh water mixes with the Gulf of Mexico and the Atlantic Ocean.

Along the southwest coast north to the Anclote Keys is a low-energy mangrove shoreline. From the Anclote Keys north around the Big Bend to the Ochlockonee River, salt marshes rim the giant estuary that receives fresh water from several springs and small rivers.

The Panhandle coast, like that of the east coast, also has a high-energy shoreline of barrier islands with bays or sounds clustered behind them. Estuaries in this region are fed with freshwater flow from several major rivers, including the Apalachicola River, Choctawhatchee River, and Escambia River, as well as many smaller rivers and springs.

Coral Reefs

The Keys boast the only living, tropical coral reefs in the continental waters of the United States. These coral gardens are a colorful matrix of bank reefs and patch reefs that stretches from Soldier Key in Biscayne National Park to the Dry Tortugas, approximately sixty miles west of Key West. Hard and soft corals, sponges, and calcareous algae vie for space on a limestone structure formed by previous generations of hard coral.

Hard corals, otherwise known as stony corals because of their external limestone skeleton, are the primary builders of the reef and include elkhorn, staghorn, star, and brain corals. Octocorals, which do not have a limestone skeleton and do not build reefs, include sea whips, sea plumes, sea fans, gorgonians, and soft corals. In all, some thirty-four species of coral have been identified on individual reefs in the Keys.

Other types of reefs thrive in Florida's warm coastal waters as well: worm reefs, vermetid reefs, *Oculina* (ivory tree coral) banks, and deep coral banks that lie on the edge of the continental slope at depths ranging from 1,320 to 2,640 feet. Worm reefs, formed by sandy tubes constructed by a tropical marine worm, are found off the east coast of Florida from Cape Canaveral to Key Biscayne. Vermetid reefs, formed by a wormlike mollusk, occur in the intertidal zone seaward of the outermost islands in the Ten Thousand Islands. Reefs of ivory tree coral thrive on underlying limestone ridges off the east coast from Jacksonville south to the St. Lucie Inlet in about three hundred feet of water. Deep-water coral banks are found off both the east and west coasts of Florida.

Chapter 3

The Panhandle

The landscape of the Florida Panhandle is dominated by rolling hills that gradually slope toward the Gulf of Mexico, a product of streams and waves acting upon the terrain over the last ten million to fifteen million years. Three of Florida's largest rivers—the Apalachicola, Choctawhatchee, and Escambia—wend their way toward the Gulf, nourished by hundreds of smaller creeks and seeps. Along some rivers, high bluffs overlook wooded floodplains, and much of the landscape is carpeted with forests of hardwoods more reminiscent of those of the southern Appalachians than other areas of Florida. The Panhandle also harbors the state's largest longleaf pine forests—sandhill, clayhill, and flatwoods—which in some places are pocked by acidic bogs that bristle with pitcher plants and other carnivorous plants. Over thousands of years, underground rivers have carved an extensive labyrinth of limestone caverns that in some areas are filled with bats, blind crayfish, and salamanders.

Facing page: *The Waterfall Room, with its array of columns, soda straws, and other formations, is one of the most striking chambers in the Florida Cavern at Florida Caverns State Park. Visitors to caves should never touch the formations because oil from fingertips will inhibit the continued development of the formations.*
Above: *An eastern pipistrelle, Florida's smallest bat, hangs from the roof of a cave. It is generally solitary and roosts in Spanish moss and under leaves, as well as in caves, especially in winter.*

Florida Caverns State Park is nestled in the heart of the Marianna Lowlands, a hilly region riddled with caverns in the eastern Panhandle. The park has one large cave, the Florida Cavern, open year-round for ranger-led tours; it also has several smaller caves closed to the public to protect their natural features, including the endangered gray bats that hibernate in the caves. Trails lead visitors through a hardwood forest and up the low bluffs bordering a section of the Chipola River floodplain, passing by limestone boulders and outcrops as well as caverns.

It was to the Florida Cavern that I followed a ranger down a path to the door at the cave's entrance as late afternoon light burned gold into the limbs and autumn leaves of the trees overhead. Each of us wore a headlamp with fresh batteries, and I was lugging camera gear to photograph the cave's interior.

As we entered the cavern and the ranger closed the door behind us, we were immediately engulfed by darkness without a glimmer of light anywhere. We flipped on headlamps long enough to find the switches that provide room-by-room lighting for visitors to view the cave's formations. The names of the cave chambers in the cavern run the gamut from silly to sumptuous—Wedding Room (named for a formation resembling a wedding cake), Donald Duck Room, the Catacombs, South America Room, Vanilla Fudge Room, Waterfall Room, and the Cathedral Room. Other named features in the cave, including Midnight Mountain, Carrot Patch, Rock Forest, and Wahoo Crawl, were no doubt the stuff of the imaginations of the spelunkers who first mapped them. The normal cave tour lasts about forty-five minutes, but my cameras necessitated a more leisurely pace that consumed the better part of three hours. I had ample time to gaze in awe at splendid calcite formations of stalactites and stalagmites, columns and soda straws, rimstones and flowstones and ribbon rock—the culmination of thousands of years of interaction between dripping mineral-laden water and air within the cave.

Air-filled caves, or terrestrial caves, are generally considered dry aquatic caverns because all caverns initially develop under aquatic conditions. Air-filled caves are rare in Florida, except in north Florida and the Panhandle, particularly in the Marianna Lowlands. The high number of air-filled caves in this region is because the water table is lower than the upper passageways of the caverns, allowing them to fill with air rather than water.

According to Richard Franz from the Florida Museum of Natural History, a cave undergoes two phases of development. The first phase involves the formation of the cave space itself, which occurs entirely underwater as the result of the interaction between water and carbon dioxide to form carbonic acid, changing the chemical nature of the limestone bedrock. All caves in Florida are formed in limestone, and they all go through this dissolution process. When the water table drops below a part of the cave, the chambers and passageways in that area fill with air, and enlargement of the space stops.

This process prompts the second phase of development, which occurs when the cave is dry. Water laden with calcium minerals trickles into the cavern from the surface, and as these minerals are deposited inside the cave, they calcify into stalagmites, stalactites, and the other formations that make caverns so interesting. If the water table rises to once again flood the cave, the enlargement phase begins anew.

Cave Zones

In many air-filled caves, especially longer ones, there are three zones: a twilight zone, middle zone, and deep zone. Relative to these zones are corresponding populations of animals and, in the twilight zone, a few plants. Vegetation is scant in caves because natural light decreases rapidly within several feet of the cave's mouth. The extent to which light penetrates the cave is the twilight zone, which may contain a few species of algae, mosses, liverworts, and an occasional fern or herbaceous plant.

Beyond the twilight zone, visible, non-animal life

is basically limited to a few small fungi that grow on guano or other organic material. The twilight zone experiences greater fluctuations in humidity and temperature than do other zones of the cave. Temperature and humidity are more stable in the middle zone—a dark region in which air still circulates—and the deep zone, which occurs in the farthest reaches of long caves. The deep zone is the most stable of cave zones because not even the air moves.

Temperatures remain relatively constant at 69–73°F in Florida's caves throughout the year because thick limestone walls buffer the interior from the extremes of outside conditions. This, and the shelter that caves provide, make them popular homes for many animals, including three species of bats.

Florida has twelve resident species of bats, all of which are night-flying insect eaters, but only the endangered gray bat, the southeastern bat, and the eastern pipistrelle roost in caves. The gray bat's range in Florida is limited to areas around caves in Jackson County, where Florida Caverns State Park is lo-

cated. This species hibernates in large colonies during the winter. In the breeding season, females give birth and raise their young in "maternity" caves, preferring to roost over standing water. During this time, single females and males roost in separate caves (called "bachelor" caves) from mothers with young. The southeastern bat also raises its young in maternity caves. The eastern pipistrelle, Florida's smallest bat, is generally solitary and roosts in Spanish moss and under leaves, as well as in caves, especially in winter.

Other animals besides bats make their homes in caves as well. An eastern woodrat often will build a nest just inside the mouth of a cave, typically under large rocks or crevices in the walls. Salamanders are common in caves, and during my trip into Florida Cavern, I found a young slimy salamander, one of three species that wander into Florida caves. Camel crickets frequent the twilight zone and dark zones, along with cave millipedes and cave spiders.

The eastern woodrat, many bats, a few salamanders, and cave crickets are examples of troxoglenes, creatures that spend much of their time in caves, but must return to the surface to feed and breed. They generally limit their activities to the twilight and middle zones. Troglobites (phreatobites in aquatic caves) are creatures that spend their entire lives in caves, including eating and reproducing. They can survive in total darkness and live in the deepest regions of caves. Most troglobites feed on detritus and fecal matter, all of which comes from animals that periodically venture outside caves to feed. Vision is useless in the dark, thus many troglobites are blind, including blind cave crayfish, blind cave salamanders, cave amphipods, cave shrimp, cave snails, and cave isopids—all present in underwater caverns. Arthropods such as cave mites, cave spiders and springtails, and a cave earwig thrive in terrestrial caves in northern Florida.

Hardwood Hammocks and Steepheads

The delicate and beautiful caverns of Florida Caverns State Park are not the park's sole attraction. I have taken many long walks through lush hardwood forests, admiring the first wildflowers of spring (in January), cursing the swarming mosquitoes of summer, and humbled by the blaze of colors of leaves in fall. Much of the terrain covering the caverns and many other areas of the northern Panhandle is cloaked with southern magnolia, American beech, sweet gum, spruce pine, pignut hickory, American holly, laurel oak, white oak, swamp chestnut oak, hop-hornbeam, ironwood, and dogwood. Shrubs and small trees such as wild-olive, sparkleberry, witch-hazel, fringe-tree, horse-sugar, strawberry-bush, and redbay are abundant, although ground-hugging herbaceous species are not because so little light reaches the forest floor. Thick vines of muscadine grapes, spiked catbrier, and poison ivy drape from understory trees and shrubs. Hammocks dominated by southern magnolia and American beech are considered the climax forest of the Panhandle.

Many Panhandle hammocks trace their origins to the Miocene Epoch and rival the cove forests of the Appalachian Mountains in diversity of species. These hammocks are unique among southeastern hardwood forests in that they harbor endemic trees, including the endangered torreya and Florida yew. Several species of animals and plants, including delicate wildflowers such as trillium, columbine, bellwort, and rue anemone, reach the southern terminus of their range in these hardwood hammocks, adding to the interesting commingling of temperate, subtropical, and endemic life forms that make these forests like no other.

Photosynthesis in hardwood forests occurs primarily high in the canopy. The animals that consume the buds, leaves, flowers, fruits, and nuts live most of their lives in the treetops and include gray squirrels and flying squirrels, as well as vireos, warblers, woodpeckers, and other birds dependent on arboreal insects. In contrast, the food web of the forest floor is based on leaves, sticks, twigs, flower parts, and seeds. As this tree litter accumulates on the forest floor, it is consumed by a host of ground-dwelling invertebrates, including springtails, mites, harvestmen, beetles, hemipterans, millipedes, dipterans, isopods, orthopterans, and earthworms. These creatures in turn are prey to spiders, predatory insects, reptiles, amphibians, and birds.

Although Florida as a whole is remarkably flat, the northern tier of the Panhandle is not. Rivers and streams have carved an undulating landscape of bluffs and deep ravines, profoundly influencing the hardwood forests of this region and the distribution of species among them. As a case in point, the nature of the terrain has given rise to a type of hardwood forest known only in Florida—the steephead. Steepheads are found in the deep Pleistocene sands of the Cody Scarp, a geological demarcation separating the clay-rich Miocene soils along the extreme northern edge of the Panhandle from the more recently emerged well-drained Pleistocene sands that slope gently towards the Gulf of Mexico. They are aligned in an east-west direction, suggesting an ancient shoreline.

Steephead forests and their stream valleys are formed by groundwater leaking downslope through porous sand at the head of a stream catchment. On the top of the slopes where vegetation is exposed to wind and extremes in temperature and moisture, longleaf pine–scrub oak communities or sparse forests of mockernut hickory and deciduous, xeric oaks dominate. Mid-slope you find forest similar to the beech-magnolia climax, while on the moist, protected lower third of slopes shaded from the sun by either their northern exposure or the depth of the ravine, an evergreen shrub zone holds sway.

It is in this evergreen shrub zone, particularly in steepheads of the Apalachicola River basin, that you find rare endemics such as the torreya and Florida yew, as well as disjunct populations of northern plants. The torreya and the Florida yew are well-adapted to the chronic disturbance inherent with life on a sandy slope. Individual plants slide downslope as a result of shifting sand. Their stems may fall over, but will then root and produce new upright stems. A single plant may be long-lived, but is likely to shift location along a slope. The largest plants are most

Trumpets and spring wildflowers spread into a pine flatwoods community at Apalachicola National Forest.

often found on the lower slopes where conditions are more stable, while the smaller plants live farther upslope.

At the bottom of the ravine, where there is almost constantly a thin flow of water, wetland plants and animals thrive. Almost every steephead supports breeding populations of dusky, two-lined and red salamanders that feed on the abundant arthropods living on the leaf litter of the stream valley floor.

Succession, a one-way metamorphosis in the composition of an ecosystem as competing organisms (particularly plants) respond to and modify their environment, is rare in hardwood forests and generally occurs only when overstory trees fall, creating gaps in the canopy. Many canopy hardwoods are clonal, meaning that they may resprout from roots or downed trunks if damaged. In these species, which include magnolia, sour gum, and sweet gum, individual trees may be long-lived, and new saplings rarely reach maturity under the deep shade of the canopy.

Considering the fierce competition among plants in the understory and forest floor, I asked Dr. Sharon Hermann of Tall Timbers Research Station near Tallahassee to explain the impact of gaps in Panhandle hammocks. According to Hermann, gaps are important not only because a crown has been blown out of the canopy from one or more trees, but because it significantly changes the environmental characteristics of the forest floor. Light is increased, humidity fluctuates more dramatically, and slow-growing tree species such as beech and white oak that typically germinate and grow as young trees in deep shade experience a tremendous growth spurt. For some trees, gaps are so important for the survival of saplings that the species may die out if a hurricane, fire, or other disturbance does not tear a hole in the canopy and allow sunlight to flood the forest floor.

Spruce pine is a classic example of a gap-dependent species in Panhandle hardwood forests. It is a short-lived but fast-growing tree that needs a tremendous influx of light (such as that which can occur only from a big gap, typically the result of several trees coming down) in order for its seedlings to germinate and survive. Until Hurricane Kate came through in 1985, Woodyard Hammock, owned and studied extensively by Tall Timbers, was down to about a dozen large, old spruce pines, with no younger trees to speak of. Without the hurricane, there would have been a chance of the spruce pine disappearing naturally in this hammock, a situation somewhat similar to that of the lignum vitae trees on Lignumvitae Key in the Keys, which are being shaded out by taller tropical canopy species. Thanks to the hurricane, Woodyard Hammock has many young spruce pines.

Gaps create a temporal and spatial mosaic in the forest, and the size of the gaps affect their impact on the surrounding vegetation. Some gaps may grow by chance as surrounding trees fall without their neighbors to buffer them. If a gap is small, the trees surrounding it may lean in and fill the space, so new trees will not take the place of those that fell. The filling in of a gap may occur within a few years, but a gap's tenure depends upon its size and what happens after it was created—for example, if high winds widened the gap or a fast-growing tree grew up through the center, closing it off.

The dynamic nature of gaps may in part affect how the many species of hardwoods in Panhandle hammocks maintain themselves. Many different species specialize in various combinations of light and shade. The hammocks are diverse not only in the variety of trees in the forest canopy, but also in understory species. In a dynamic forest, there are plenty of niches for many species—plants and animals. Some birds specialize in gaps, while others avoid gaps altogether. Gaps often create an environment in which there is much flowering and fruiting. For example, dogwoods flower and produce fruit in people's yards, but they do so rarely in their natural setting. When they do, it is because they are getting increased sunlight along the edge of some kind of disturbance, such as a gap. Weedy species such as wild grape and poison ivy also proliferate in these conditions.

Pine Flatwoods

Pine flatwoods in the Panhandle generally claim purchase between sandhill communities, which lie upslope, and evergreen shrub and pitcher plant bogs downslope. Most of these forests are dominated by longleaf pine, but in others slash pine, pond pine,

combustible fuel that when sparked by lightning, and later by people, roused a fire that might spread unchecked for miles over flat or gently rolling flatwoods. Fires that occurred every three or four years effectively eliminated the chance of hardwoods growing taller than small shrubs. This ensured an open pine canopy beneath which yellow foxglove, dwarf huckleberry, blazing star, saw palmetto, gallberry, runner oaks, ground huckleberry, bracken fern, and more than two hundred species of groundcover plants prospered. Groundwater is usually much nearer the surface than in other pine communities, resulting in lush vegetative growth. This in turn fuels a diverse wildlife community, including salamanders, frogs, lizards, snakes, rabbits, native rats and mice, whitetailed deer, bobcat, gray fox, and black bear.

Perhaps the most famous pine flatwood residents are the red-cockaded woodpeckers, or RCWs as they are called by those who study and admire them. Once common throughout the Southeast, the woodpeckers are now endangered because of loss or degradation of old-growth pine habitat. Red-cockaded woodpeckers are not particularly picky about the type of pine they colonize, choosing longleaf,

or a mix of the three species may be prevalent. The longleaf pine-wiregrass community is believed to have been the most substantial forest type before the arrival of Europeans, originally covering an estimated twenty-four million acres from Mobile Bay, Alabama, east throughout Florida and north through the Coastal Plain in Georgia. Although the total acreage of longleaf flatwoods has been significantly reduced, vast expanses still stretch east to west between the Ochlockonee and Choctawhatchee Rivers and north to south between the Cody Scarp and the Panhandle Gulf Coast.

Fire was the guardian of these forests; dropped longleaf needles and wiregrass provided a highly

loblolly, shortleaf, slash, or pond, but they must have mature *living* trees in which to hammer out cavities for roosting and nesting (unlike other birds that typically excavate cavities in snags).

Red-cockaded woodpeckers in Florida range from the Panhandle down to Big Cypress Swamp in south Florida. Their greatest strongholds, however, are in the Apalachicola National Forest and on Eglin Air Force Base—both in the Panhandle. They are small birds, about seven inches long, mostly white on the breast and undersides with a black-and-white laddered back and a large white cheek patch. The cockade, a small patch of scarlet feathers above the white cheek patch on males, is rarely shown unless the bird is excited.

Red-cockaded woodpeckers are extremely social and live in groups of up to nine birds centered around one breeding pair. Young non-breeding males from previous broods stay around the cavity as "helpers" to the breeding adults, assisting in the incubation of eggs, feeding young, making new cavities, and defending the clan's territory from other red-cockaded woodpeckers. Young females virtually never serve as helpers, and they are the ones to disperse, usually within two miles of their birth cavity. They look for single males with no dominant female. Unattached females stay on the fringes of other territories, constantly probing for an opening. If one bird of a breeding pair dies, pairs in adjacent territories check out the situation, and if there is a helper male or young female available, that young bird will take the place of the deceased breeder.

A single group's territory may cover one hundred acres or more of pine forest mixed with small-to-medium-sized hardwoods. Most of the territory is used as foraging area around the group's cluster of cavity trees. One to as many as twelve trees may be used for cavities at any one time by the woodpeckers. Cavities are typically excavated in live, mature pines infected with red heart disease, a common heart rot fungus that causes a softening of pine heartwood. Most pines are only susceptible to the

fungus when they are more than sixty years old. For longleaf, the minimum age for red-cockaded woodpecker colonization is approximately ninety years. Red-cockaded woodpeckers prefer infected trees because the softened heartwood makes cavity excavation easier. Cavities within the colony may be in various stages of completion: some may be occupied, some are under construction, and still others have been abandoned. The woodpeckers invest a lot of time—up to a year—in excavating cavities, which makes them quite valuable to the birds.

An active hole can be distinguished from one that has been abandoned by the broad, chalky-white resin slick that stains the face of the tree roughly ten feet below and above the cavity. Red-cockaded woodpeckers tap wells into the trees to maintain a constant stream of sticky sap as protection against predators, such as rat snakes or flying squirrels. This is one reason they require living trees as opposed to dead snags. If the sap dries out, the hole becomes accessible to predators. Woodpeckers will also abandon a tree if the understory of hardwoods grows to the level of the cavity. Again, this serves to prevent predation because tall hardwoods become ladders for predators, especially flying squirrels, to reach woodpecker holes and consume eggs or young. It is essential to the clan's survival that enough mature pines are available to be used for cavity trees as existing cavity trees die or are abandoned.

RCW conservation is an issue as sticky as the sap that runs down the woodpeckers' doorsteps. Most important to red-cockaded woodpeckers is the number of cavity trees or potential cavity trees. So much of the southeastern pine forests was clear-cut in the early 1900s that the birds are basically living in relict scraps of habitat. Says Dr. Todd Engstrom, an ornithologist from Tall Timbers, "The habitat you see RCWs in now is largely a reflection of what was left, not what they chose. The birds had no choice. They are using the best of the remaining habitat, and in many cases, it is poor. But they have been able to get by. The question now is whether they will be able to

The flowers of pitcher plants, such as this purple pitcher plant, are pollinated by bumblebees. The long, tubular leaves of these plants—the pitchers—are produced each year from underground rhizomes or roots and act as pitfalls for unwary insects or tiny animals attracted by nectar secreted by glands near the mouth of the pitcher.

make it through their current population bottleneck until the trees get older—if the trees are allowed to get older."

Many landowners want to clear-cut their timber as it becomes mature rather than cut it selectively, which eliminates any chance of red-cockaded woodpeckers being able to remain on the land—and few other animals as well. That preference, and continued resistance by some private landowners to prescribed burning as a way to maintain quality pine habitat, spells trouble for red-cockaded woodpeckers. For these reasons, Engstrom is pessimistic about the birds' chances on private land in Florida and Georgia. He thinks the woodpeckers' best chance of recovery will be on public lands, where the Endangered Species Act is enforced more rigorously and where the forests are not as fragmented as those on private lands.

Pitcher Plant Bogs

Among my favorite places to visit in the Panhandle are the sunken, soggy spots amidst the pine forests where carnivorous plants lurk. These are commonly known as pitcher plant bogs and include pitcher plants, sundews, badderworts, and butterworts

Above: *A stream running through a sandhill community tumbles sixty-five feet down the face of this sinkhole, creating the waterfall at Falling Waters State Recreation Area.*

Left: *The Nature Conservancy's Apalachicola Bluffs and Ravines Preserve provides many fine views of the Apalachicola River and its floodplain forest from high bluffs along the river. It is on steep, shaded slopes near the Apalachicola River that you find rare endemics such as the torreya and Florida yew, as well as disjunct populations of northern plants.*

among the carnivorous residents. Most pitcher plant bogs are fairly small, but in the western half of Apalachicola National Forest, some are so extensive they form vast treeless plains known as savannas. Based on accounts by William Bartram in the 1700s, areas near the coast from Pensacola west to Pascagoula, Mississippi, were practically continuous bogs, with individual savannas covering thousands of acres. Few such bogs remain today, and even fewer have been left in their natural state—victims of drainage for agricultural activity and fire suppression. Other factors contributing to the decline of bog habitat include conversion of bogs to farm ponds, urban sprawl, highway construction, and herbicide use.

Pitcher plant bogs, so named because pitcher plants are the most characteristic species, rarely flood, but they remain perpetually wet except during extreme drought. The bogs' carnivorous inhabitants depend on frequent fires to help eliminate competition from encroaching hardwood shrubs. Scientists theorize that many bog plants resort to carnivory to supplement what few nutrients and minerals they obtain from the relatively barren, acidic soil in which they live.

Pitcher plants in Florida are all members of the genus *Sarracenia*. They produce large, beautiful flowers of red or yellow (depending on species) in spring and are pollinated by bumblebees. Many pitchers have hoods to deflect rainwater. The long, tubular leaves of these plants—the pitchers—grow each year from underground rhizomes or roots and act as pitfalls for unwary insects or other tiny animals attracted by nectar secreted by glands near the mouth of the pitcher. The interior surface of the pitcher bristles with downward-pointing hairs that help prevent prey from escaping the plant's digestive juices. According to Dr. George Folkerts in a 1982 *American Scientist* article, carnivorous plants sharing the same habitat specialize in different animal foods to avoid competition, something he calls "prey partitioning." For example, *S. minor*, the hooded pitcher plant, seems to catch mainly ants, while *S. purpurea*, the purple pitcher plant, feasts on grasshoppers, crickets, and snails—a smorgasbord of organisms quite different from that consumed by other pitcher plants.

Some creatures, however, have turned the tables on pitcher plants by evolving to survive within the pitcher and take advantage of a unique microclimate found nowhere else in nature. According to Folkerts, the interior of the pitcher leaves is generally higher in relative humidity than the surrounding environment, somewhat less variable in temperature, and fairly dim. Furthermore, there is free food for the taking—the mass of trapped organisms decomposing inside the pitcher. Among the creatures that inhabit pitchers without being trapped or digested are a species of mosquito, several flies, moths, aphids, and mites. At least fourteen species of arthropods are pitcher plant obligates, meaning that they cannot survive without pitcher plants.

The other carnivorous plants in bogs are somewhat less conspicuous than the pitcher plants, but are equally fascinating. Bladderworts, which can live in water or on land, have no roots, but instead dispatch small insects and protozoans with tiny, fluid-filled bladders that literally suck in prey. Sundews, which glisten like tiny rubies, have small leaves coated with sticky droplets resembling dew. When an insect attracted to the droplets lands on a leaf, it becomes stuck as if to flypaper and is digested.

A Landscape of Inspired Splendor

The Florida Panhandle is a region of singular beauty and an astounding variety of ecosystems and unusual species. Its ancient connections to the Appalachians make it unlike any other part of Florida. Yes, the Panhandle has palm trees and miles of brilliant white beaches on its Gulf Coast, but the long winding rivers, secret caves, quiet hills of burnished autumn hues, and delicate palette of spring and fall wildflowers dispel any preconceptions one might have about the sameness of Florida wilderness. The Panhandle is indeed a landscape of inspired splendor.

Overleaf: *The setting sun illuminates the limestone ledges and fall leaves of mixed hardwoods and cypress along the Chipola River floodplain, Florida Caverns State Park.*

Chapter 4

North Florida

Among the finest experiences I have had while canoeing Florida rivers has been watching wild turkeys forage along the banks. My wife, Renée, and I considered ourselves particularly lucky one morning on the Santa Fe River when we heard a wild turkey calling and then watched it fly across the river about a quarter-mile in front of us. We were even more excited to see it fly back across the river. However, when the turkey crossed a third time, we became worried. Moments later, I spotted two small turkey chicks, or poults, in the water, inching their way upstream. Before this encounter, I had no idea wild turkeys could swim, especially ones this young. The adult turkey, which at this point we assumed was the mother, flew across the river a fourth time, just in front of us, and landed on the south bank. Both poults appeared to be weakening, and the one closest to us was beginning to drift downstream. It was time for a rescue.

Facing page: *Begger-ticks, also known as marsh marigolds, created a golden mantle one fall over much of Paynes Prairie. The immense stands of flowers, which stood six feet tall in some areas, followed prescribed burns earlier in the year.*

Above: *A barking tree frog, Florida's largest native tree frog, clings to a saw palmetto frond. From a distance, the breeding chorus of these frogs sounds like barking dogs. Biologists know little about their lives away from breeding areas in cypress heads and small ponds.*

We maneuvered our canoe cross-stream toward the nearest poult, herding it toward the north bank. Our looming presence instilled new energy in the young turkey, and it wiggled vigorously along the overhang of the bank in an attempt to scramble onto shore and into cover. Renée nearly went overboard grabbing for the bird, but we finally cornered it, and she scooped it up from the front of the canoe. The poult struggled for a moment, but calmed quickly in the warmth of her hands. I turned the canoe and aimed for the south shore where we had last seen the mother, anticipating the need to pick up the second poult en route. But it had other ideas and managed to work its way over toward the south bank, scrambling up the steep slope toward the forest as our canoe approached.

Now we spotted the mother and possibly six other poults waiting on a ridge along the edge of the trees as the second youngster joined them. The mother paced nervously, still calling, and our bird wriggled in anticipation as we neared shore. I nosed the canoe up to the bank and Renée released the poult, a smile spreading across her face when it finally reached the ridge to join the other turkeys. After a couple of minutes, the family descended the ridge and melted into the forest.

Springs

Many north Florida rivers, including the Santa Fe, Ichetucknee, and Suwannee, either originate as springs or receive inflow from springs somewhere along their course. The Ichetucknee River bubbles up from springs within Ichetucknee Springs State Park, eventually merging with the Santa Fe, a major tributary of the Suwannee. The Suwannee begins as a blackwater river in Georgia's Okefenokee Swamp, meandering southwest some two hundred and fifty miles before it empties into the Gulf of Mexico just north of the Cedar Keys. Along the length of the Suwannee, more than fifty springs contribute to the river's flow, with an additional fifty contributing to the river's tributaries—the Santa Fe, Withlacoochee, and Alapaha Rivers.

The springs are renowned for their clarity and relatively constant year-round temperatures. On the Santa Fe, Renée and I could look over the side of our canoe in several feet of water, trailing our fingers through tapering strands of tape grass billowing in the current, convinced the bottom and multitudes of fish beneath us were only inches from our grasp. The water is clear in springs and in spring-fed rivers (calcareous streams) because it has been filtered through limestone bedrock that in places is more than ten thousand feet thick. The clarity of spring water is responsible for the azure color of deeper springs—similar to that of a cloudless winter sky—because the clear water differentially filters the wavelengths of sunlight streaming down through the water column, leaving only the blue wavelength of the spectrum visible. Spring water is less acidic than water in other rivers, and it differs chemically as well, containing ions of calcium, magnesium, iron, and other minerals. It varies little in temperature near its source at the spring head because of its underground origin. Normally, the bottom of a spring is exposed limestone or limestone covered by a layer of sand.

Clear water combined with low acidity and constant, moderate temperatures create conditions ideal for aquatic plants, including tape grass, wild rice, giant cutgrass, arrowheads, southern naiads, pondweeds, and chara. Florida's springs are among the most productive aquatic systems in the world because of the prolific vegetation, and they are home to dozens of species of fish, turtles, snakes, mollusks, and insects. Aquatic plants are critical to all inhabitants of springs and spring-fed rivers because they provide shelter and anchor-holds for small organisms, furnish food for other creatures, and produce oxygen—so much oxygen, in fact, that on sunny days, billions of tiny bubbles may emanate from the leaves of aquatic plants and rise to the surface, clouding the normally translucent water.

William Bartram saw several springs during his travels through Florida in the mid-1700s and was enthralled by their quiet beauty and connection to aquatic caverns: "Behold now at still evening, the sun yet streaking the embroidered savannas, armies of

Bald cypress and maples overhang Manatee Springs, one of the many springs that flow into the Suwannee River. William Bartram was impressed with many of the springs he saw in Florida, describing one as a "grand pellucid fountain."

A Florida black bear emerges from a stand of oaks and pines. Less than 1,500 wild black bears are thought to remain in Florida. (Photo © Barry Mansell)

fish were pursuing their pilgrimage to the grand pellucid fountain; and when here arrived, all quiet and peaceable, encircling the little cerulean hemisphere, they descend into the dark caverns of the earth; where, probably, they are separated from each other, by innumerable paths, or secret rocky avenues; and . . . after many days absence from the surface of the world emerge again from the dreary vaults . . . sporting in the transparent waters of some far distant lake."

By contrast with Bartram's "pellucid fountains" and "cerulean hemispheres," some Florida springs are noted for their greenish color and "rotten egg" smell, the result of high sulfur content. Bartram found one of these, too, along the St. Johns River, and wrote in his journal, "This tepid water has a most disagreeable taste, brassy and vitriolic, and very offensive to the smell, much like bilge-water, or the washings of a gun barrel, and is smelt at a great distance."

Although I have never seen the spring that made such an unfavorable impression on Bartram, I have on occasion run across springs during walks through the Ocala National Forest that were murky or discolored. I was concerned at first, but read later that this was a temporary condition, typically caused by a long period of heavy rainfall or river flooding. Torrential rains may cause a spring connected through underground caverns with a nearby river to increase its flow and for a short time spew out dark, tea-colored river water. If a river overflows its banks and floods a spring, the spring may reverse its flow and create a siphon into the aquifer because the pressure of the colder river water exceeds that of the aquifer. Once the river recedes, the flow of the spring will return to normal. Sometimes a spring will discharge white, cloudy water from its mouth during periods of low rainfall—a phenomenon some scientists think results from the precipitation of dissolved limestone.

Swamps

According to Katherine C. Ewel in *Ecosystems of Florida*, there are two broad categories of swamps found in Florida. River swamps, as the name implies, occupy the floodplains of rivers, primarily in north Florida. They include whitewater floodplain forests (such as along the Apalachicola River in the Panhandle), blackwater floodplain forests (such as those along the Suwannee and Oklawaha Rivers), and spring run swamps (including those along the Wakulla, St. Marks, and Crystal Rivers). The hydroperiod is short in river swamps except where deposits of clay and organic matter retain water in depressions in the floodplain.

Stillwater swamps are fed by groundwater and rainfall. In these swamps, the flow of water is barely perceptible, and the hydroperiod is generally longer than that of river swamps. Stillwater swamps include hydric hammocks, cypress swamps, bay swamps, shrub bogs, and gum ponds.

North Florida is rich with swamps, many of which are protected in state parks, national forests, national wildlife refuges, or conservation areas managed by regional water management districts. Other areas have been purchased for conservation by private organizations such as The Nature Conservancy. By 1991, the Florida Chapter of The Nature Conservancy alone had acquired more than 141,000 acres of riverine and wetland habitat, most of which was transferred to state, federal, or regional agencies for management.

One of The Nature Conservancy's most notable purchases in north Florida was several thousand acres of Pinhook Swamp to create a wildlife corridor linking Okefenokee Swamp in Georgia with Osceola National Forest. Pinhook Swamp is noted for its mosaic of wetland communities, including pine pocosins, wet flatwoods, freshwater marshes, gum-cypress stands, and blackwater swamps. It is home to beaver, southeastern weasel, southern mink, and river otter, as well as breeding populations of sandhill crane, herons, egrets, and ibis. Biologists hope it will be a suitable location for the reintroduction of the Florida panther to Pinhook Swamp.

To the south of Pinhook Swamp is Big Gum Swamp in Osceola National Forest. It is a magnificent, boggy, wild land, and much of it a national wilderness area. Big Gum Swamp is dominated by a gum-cypress swamp in its interior and pine flatwoods on the perimeter. Water flows slowly through sloughs like dark ink, eventually forming small creeks.

My first hike into Big Gum Swamp was during the spring to look for black bear, just as a cold front was pushing through. Dark clouds glowered overhead as I wandered down an old tram road in the late afternoon, finding plenty of birds, rosebud orchids, and pitcher plants, but no bear. Much of the pine flatwoods had been recently burned, so new growth glimmered in the dim light. I hiked out in near darkness, vowing to return and possibly camp. The next morning, I arrived at the trailhead somewhat dismayed after having passed two road-killed wild hogs within a quarter mile of each other. I have no fondness for hogs because they are not native to Florida and they destroy many plants while rooting around for bulbs and tender young shoots, but I hate seeing any animal killed by traffic.

My mood was glum, and the heavy cloud cover didn't help. Thunder cracked overhead, and as I started down the trail, rain began to fall in torrents. Weather like this was fit for neither man nor bear. As I stood there in the downpour, I noticed a pair of deer staring at me from a thicket. For a few moments, we gazed into each others' eyes, dripping in the wet,

before they vanished as quietly as they had appeared. I smiled and walked back to the truck. The day was going to be okay after all.

Although soaked by the rain, I still wanted to explore, so I drove along the perimeter roads surrounding the wilderness area. After several miles, I stopped on a bridge to look at the sluggish trickle known as the middle prong of the St. Marys River. This section of the St. Marys creeps west through Big Gum Swamp until it eventually loses itself in the sloughs and meanders of creeks that finger their way through cypress, black gum, cedar, black willow, pond pine and slash pine, and titi. Stands of cypress border the river in places.

Cypress are related to the redwoods and sequoias of California. They are unusual among Florida conifers because they are deciduous, losing their feathery needles by the end of November and bursting forth with new growth in March. Bald cypress and pond cypress, the two species in Florida, are probably the most common wetland trees in swamps throughout the state, particularly those with regularly fluctuating water levels. Bald cypress grows best near rivers and in swamps with flowing water, whereas pond cypress is most likely to be found along the edges of lakes and in flatwoods ponds and swamps with little water movement.

I am often asked about the purpose of the unusual "knees" characteristic of both pond cypress and bald cypress. Cypress knees—narrow, knobby, vertical extensions of the root system—resemble monks at prayer, particularly in low light. They range in height from a few inches to a few feet, and according to some sources, may help support the tree, as well as enable it to cope with low oxygen levels in the mud or water at the roots. Both the height of the knees and that of the swollen buttress of the trunk are thought to be directly related to the average level of the water in which the tree stands, but this has not yet been proven. According to Dr. Peter Pritchard of the Florida Audubon Society, a root with "knees" is probably harder to dislodge when the tree is exposed to hurricane-force winds. A simple root can be pulled through the muck much more easily. Cypress knees are higher than they need to be because they don't "know" when they have reached the surface, so they keep growing.

Above: *Saw palmettos bristle under an open canopy of slash pines in the Big Gum Swamp Wilderness Area, Osceola National Forest.*
Left: *A barred owl looks down from a cypress at the edge of Cross Creek, namesake of a small community that was the longtime home of Marjorie Kinnan Rawlings, author of* The Yearling *and* Cross Creek.
Facing page: *Blue flag iris brightens a stand of cypress along the River Styx, near Cross Creek.*

A clear sky and the forest canopy are reflected on the surface of a flooded sinkhole at San Felasco Hammock State Preserve. Sinkholes are a prominent feature of the karst terrain that covers much of the northern half of Florida.

Most of the people I know who visit swamps on a regular basis are bird-watchers, and for good reason. Swamps furnish food and water, offer refuge, and for many species, provide nesting sites. Of the sixty-eight birds listed as rare and endangered in Florida, twelve are found in swamps. Mississippi kites and swallow-tailed kites breed only in swamps. Three species of woodpecker are known to nest in cypress or hardwood swamps, including the pileated woodpecker, the largest woodpecker seen with any frequency in North America (the similar ivory-billed woodpecker is larger, but is feared extinct because of loss of habitat). Pileated woodpeckers are unmistakable because of their large size and distinctive black and white plumage with scarlet crest. Even when they are hidden by foliage as they look for insects on branches high in the canopy, their cries of *wucka-wucka-wucka* and their resounding hammering echo through the swamp.

At dawn, the swamp is alive with bird song and flitting, feathered bodies. Birds are particularly abundant during spring and fall migrations because there is plenty of food. Warblers of all kinds fill the trees, including the northern parula, prothonotary warbler, hooded warbler, ovenbird, yellow-rumped warbler (known affectionately as "butter butt" by birders), pine warbler, and common yellowthroat. In the spring, cypress swamps often accommodate rookeries of wood storks and at least nine species of wading birds. I consider myself particularly fortunate if I get a good look at a pair of wood ducks before they launch from a secluded stretch of backwater, squeaking in panic. Wood ducks are the only species of waterfowl that nests in Florida swamps.

Other animals besides birds can be seen on a regular basis. Raccoons, river otters, and whitetailed deer are common throughout the year. The Florida black bear, on the other hand, is much more elusive. I have yet to see one, although I have come across plenty of tracks, some only minutes old. But there is good reason for them to be secretive: Until recently, they were legally hunted, in spite of their small surviving population (estimated at less than 1,500 in the state) and threatened status. A male black bear weighs between two hundred and fifty and three hundred and fifty pounds, while females top out at around two hundred pounds. When a black bear stands on its hind legs, it can reach a height of nearly seven feet. Most black bears wander a territory ranging from twenty-five to one hundred square miles, sometimes roaming twenty miles a night in search of food.

Black bears are omnivorous, meaning that they will eat almost anything. They love honey, berries, and insects, as well as nuts, fruit, and carrion. Occasionally, they will kill a wild hog or deer. In north Florida, bears feed heavily on berries in the summer, including many swamp species, such as black gum, gallberry, and needle palm. During the winter, they enter a dormant period lasting several weeks, seeking palmetto thickets or similar areas with dense growths of vegetation in which to make huge nests of leaves and pine needles. Although their heart rate, metabolism, and body temperature drop during winter denning, black bears do not truly hibernate. They may lose up to 25 percent of their weight over the winter. By spring they are ravenous.

Sandhills

After several days of exploring swamps, I am always ready to head for high, dry ground. Much of the uplands in north Florida, including that along rivers such as the Santa Fe and Ichetucknee, is occupied by longleaf sandhill communities, in which

longleaf pine, turkey oak, and wiregrass are the dominant plants. Relatively frequent fires, most of which are controlled ones set by biologists during the late spring through summer, promote a surprisingly diverse assemblage of species, considering the paucity of nutrients in the sandy soil. At Gold Head Branch State Park, for example, the sandhills support seventy-two species of herbaceous plants, including wildflowers and grasses such as golden aster, green eyes, summer farewell, splitbeard bluestem, honeycomb head, blazing star, clammey weed, and dog tongue. Spring and fall bring high color to recently burned sandhills with profuse displays of wildflowers, and as autumn turns to winter, wiregrass blooms in golden waves that appear to wash across the sand.

Biologists know that fire is paramount to the blooming of wiregrass, but little is known about how it sprouts from seed or reproduces vegetatively. It spreads so slowly that once eradicated from an area, it is unlikely ever to return. Wiregrass is remarkably long-lived, so much so that one researcher suggests that the wiregrass we see today "may have germinated from seeds centuries ago when earlier, post-Pleistocene climates provided the environmental conditions needed for reproduction."

One well-understood aspect of wiregrass ecology is its relationship with longleaf pine. Both longleaf pine and wiregrass are well adapted to fire—the breath of life for sandhill communities. Wiregrass is an extremely dense bunch grass, and the blades of one bunch usually overlap the blades of neighboring bunches, allowing fire to spread easily. Thousands of long, dry needles that have fallen from the longleaf overstory are sprinkled throughout the wiregrass. Both wiregrass and longleaf pine needles are quite flammable,

Left, top: *Longleaf pine, turkey oak, and wire grass dominate an old-growth sandhill community at the Ordway Preserve in Putnam County.*
Left, bottom: *Gopher tortoises may share their burrows with more than eighty different species of animals, including the endangered eastern indigo snake and rare gopher frog. Some animals, including two species of scarab beetles, live nowhere other than in active gopher tortoise burrows.*

and they can form a dense carpet that creates a highly combustible fuel easily sparked by lightning or people. Once a ground fire has crept through the sandhill, wiregrass resprouts quickly from rootstocks, while longleaf pine has adapted its entire life history to fire.

Longleaf pine is the only Florida pine that can survive fire as a seedling or sapling, with the exception of south Florida slash pine. Unlike most pines, it is long-lived, surviving up to five hundred years and requiring more than eighty years to mature. After sprouting, it lies flat, much like a clump of grass, from three to fifteen years. During this time (called the grass stage), the seedling grows a long, heavy taproot that reaches far beneath the sandy soil for moisture. When the seedling finally begins to grow in height, the stored food in the tap root helps it do so quickly. At this stage, the tree looks much like a bottlebrush, with a long, thin trunk and a mass of needles at the top. It delays putting out branches in order to concentrate all its energy into gaining height, an adaptation that minimizes the chance that its vulnerable apical buds or growing tips will be scorched by a ground fire. It also has a thick, corky bark and dense tufts of long needles surrounding its apical buds—both adaptations for withstanding heat.

In a healthy longleaf pine forest, the low carpet of wiregrass and other native herbaceous plants is so thick that in some places you can barely see your feet. Summer fires are critical for burning away this vegetation because longleaf seeds need bare soil and plenty of sunlight in order to germinate. Without these fires, the only bare ground available may be tipups from wind-thrown longleafs and small patches of soil unearthed by burrowing creatures, such as gopher tortoises, pocket gophers, and scarab beetles. In autumn the pines drop their seeds, which germinate from October to March when the seeds of other plants are dormant, essentially eliminating the need to compete with other young seedlings for nutrients and light.

The original longleaf forest that covered much of the Southeast was not only capable of surviving spring and summer fires, but may have actually helped start and sustain them, according to Steven H. Wolfe, Jeffrey A. Reidenauer, and D. Bruce Means in *An Ecological Characterization of the Florida Panhandle*. Lightning is attracted to old, large pines, which often have more resin in their heartwood than younger trees and are more likely to be afflicted by heart rot, a fungal infection that makes the heartwood porous and more flammable. Because of this, old trees are frequently set ablaze after a lightning strike and may spark a fire, despite heavy rain. Even a smoldering tree can start a ground fire in the duff and wiregrass several days after the storm has passed and the ground has dried.

On my hikes through sandhill, I occasionally see the large, deep sandy burrows of gopher tortoises. Gopher tortoises, or "gophers," are found throughout the state in dry upland habitats, mostly with pine. They are medium-sized turtles, generally measuring nine to eleven inches long and weighing eight to ten pounds as adults. Their life expectancy in the wild is long—between forty to sixty years, although it is said they may live more than one hundred and fifty years. The head is broad and stubby, the tail is relatively short, and the shell is rounded, ranging in color from tan to dark gray. Gopher tortoises use their powerful forelimbs tipped with stiff, flattened claws as shovels to excavate burrows of about fifteen feet long and six feet deep, although one burrow discovered in 1972 measured more than forty-five feet in length. The temperature within the burrow remains relatively constant throughout the year: 60°–70°F in winter and 70°–80°F in summer. The burrows are also fairly humid; gopher tortoises, unlike many other tortoises, are quite susceptible to dehydration, and some biologists think they may migrate to other burrows in moister habitats during the dry winter months.

Most of a gopher tortoise's life is spent in or around its burrow. They are creatures of habit, wearing paths through vegetation as they regularly visit the same foraging areas. Gopher tortoises are primarily vegetarians, feeding on such things as broad-leaved grasses, wiregrass, wild legumes, fallen pine needles, and various wild fruits and berries. They have also been known to eat insects and carrion—even the bones of dead tortoises.

Although gopher tortoises spend a great deal of time in their burrows, it is not a solitary existence. More than one gopher tortoise may share a burrow (at least temporarily), and eighty-one species of animals have been identified as "burrow commensals"—creatures that use tortoise burrows to varying degrees. Burrow commensals include two species of scarab beetle, the gopher cricket, whip scorpion, gopher frog, eastern indigo snake, and Florida mouse. *Aphrodius troglodytes* and *Copris gopheri*, both scarab beetles, are known as obligate burrow commensals—animals thought to live nowhere other than in active gopher tortoise burrows. Burrow commensals are drawn to gopher tortoise burrows for a number of different reasons. Some insects during certain life stages eat gopher tortoise fecal material. The gopher frog often feeds on insects and spiders that live in the burrows. The indigo snake uses tortoise burrows for winter shelter and nesting, as does the Florida mouse, which lives year-round in a den it builds along the burrow shaft. Burrows also provide tortoises and other wildlife with a safe haven when ground fires burn through sandhill or other pine habitat.

The burrowing activities of gopher tortoises benefit plants as well. The mound of sand at the mouth of a burrow provides bare soil important to the establishment of seedlings, including longleaf pine and, on the southern Lake Wales Ridge of central Florida, a threatened scrub mint, *Dicerandra frutescens*. Paths to feeding sites and favored feeding areas also create open space for seedling growth. Furthermore, because of their broad herbivorous diet, gopher tortoises help maintain the diversity of plant species near their burrows by dispersing seeds.

Sandhill is extremely dry habitat, but sometimes small, ephemeral ponds and larger, permanent lakes occur, as Dick Franz pointed out to me during a tour of an old-growth north Florida sandhill community owned jointly by the University of Florida and The Nature Conservancy. Both the lakes and the ponds are important sources of fresh water for sandhill wildlife, but the ponds are essential to many animals for another reason.

Ephemeral sandhill ponds are caused by the seepage of groundwater up through the sand. As long as the hardpan layer beneath the pond stays moist, the pond will retain water. If a pond dries down too far, aerobic action renews, and the organic hardpan begins to oxidize and break down. What water remains percolates down into the aquifer.

Because there is no way in or out of this type of pond, there are no fish, allowing amphibians to live and reproduce in a relatively predator-free environment. In a typical north Florida sandhill pond, you can expect to find tadpoles of pinewoods tree frogs, barking tree frogs, cricket frogs, bullfrogs, pig frogs, leopard frogs, and gopher frogs, as well as larval and adult striped newts. According to Franz, many of these animals breed in the ponds, but spend their adult lives in the surrounding uplands. He also thinks that because these ponds are so attractive to amphibians, aquatic insects, and other creatures, they may form prey reservoirs for upland snakes (the equivalent of a reptilian patio buffet), such as black racers, coachwhips, garter snakes, and pygmy rattlesnakes.

As I listened to Franz, I could not help but draw a parallel between the ephemeral nature of the ponds and the nature of wild north Florida. Both are rare and precious, and both are undeniably sensitive to human disturbance. When the bottom dissolves in a sandhill pond, the water disappears. So too will wild places and creatures in north Florida disappear if there is not a continuous, uncompromising effort to protect them.

A creek empties into the cypress-lined Suwannee River at Suwannee River State Park. The Suwannee begins as a blackwater river in Georgia's Okefenokee Swamp, meandering southwest some 250 miles before it empties into the Gulf of Mexico just north of the Cedar Keys.

71

Above: *A pygmy rattlesnake lies coiled in the leaf litter along the Florida Trail at Stephen Foster State Cultural Center.*
Right: *Fog lifts from an expanse of goldenrod on Paynes Prairie at Paynes Prairie State Preserve, south of Gainesville. William Bartram visited the prairie and nearby Alachua Sink in the 1770s and described them in detail in his famous journal, published in 1791 as* Travels of William Bartram.
Facing page: *An old maple hangs over the Santa Fe River at O'Leno State Park.*

Chapter 5

Central Florida

In a part of Florida known mainly for Disney World and other popular theme parks, central Florida's natural landscape has much to offer anyone interested in a quieter interlude. Hundreds of lakes dot the region. Scrub, said to be among North America's oldest ecosystems, harbors several endangered species, many of which are endemic to the Lake Wales Ridge, an ancient shoreline known as the spine of central Florida. A matrix of dry prairies, cypress swamps, temperate hardwood hammocks, flatwoods, and freshwater marshes spreads north and east from the Lake Wales Ridge. Several rivers, including the Little Manatee, Hillsborough, Wekiva, and Peace, originate in central Florida and wend their way west toward the Gulf of Mexico. The freshwater marshes that comprise the headwaters of the St. Johns River lie near the Atlantic Coast, and in the heart of central Florida, a chain of lakes forms the headwaters of the Kissimmee River, which drains into Lake Okeechobee.

Facing page: *Bald cypress rise from their reflections in a pond at Highlands Hammock State Park.*
Above: *A male black-winged damselfly pauses on the tip of a fern frond at Highlands Hammock State Park. These diminutive creatures flit slowly from perch to perch in the deep shade of hammocks, occasionally nabbing a small insect.*

Scrub

The sun had almost burned away the morning mist when I reached the jeep trail that cut through a dwarfed forest of scrubby oaks and shrubs at Archbold Biological Station, a private preserve and research facility on the southern end of the Lake Wales Ridge in Highlands County. Scattered throughout the scrub-oak forest were open grassy areas and bare patches of blinding white sand. Most of the oaks were less than four or five feet tall, but a few stood closer to ten feet, interrupting the otherwise uniform, low, green expanse. It was in the top branches of these taller trees that I scanned for a Florida scrub jay on sentinel duty.

Florida scrub jays are a federally listed threatened species restricted to arid, low-growing oak scrub habitats of peninsular Florida. It is the state's only endemic bird, meaning that it is the only bird in Florida that lives nowhere else in the world. Much of the bird's habitat, considered one of the rarest and most distinctive communities in North America, has been lost to agriculture and development. As a direct result, biologists estimate that the Florida scrub jay population has declined by more than 50 percent in the last one hundred years. But the jays are still thriving at Archbold and have been the focus of more than twenty years of intense study by biologists Glen E. Woolfenden and John W. Fitzpatrick. Their studies have revealed interesting information regarding the Florida scrub jay's social structure, and much of what is known about these birds is the result of their research at Archbold.

Florida scrub jays are similar in size and shape to blue jays, but their plumage is a more subtle blue grading to pale gray on the back and belly. Males and females cannot be distinguished from one another by their plumage.

After walking only a few minutes down the trail, I spotted a sentinel jay and called to it with several loud *psheeeps*. The surrounding oaks erupted with feathered blue and gray bodies, and I was immediately encircled by three birds, each staring up at me from the sand, expecting a handout. No peanuts here. After a few fruitless minutes, they lost interest and began to poke around in the oak leaf litter and scrub palmettos for insects. The sentinel remained vigilant from its perch while the others looked for food.

Like other jays, scrub jays have a broad diet that includes insects, spiders, tree frogs, lizards, small snakes, berries, and seeds. Their primary plant food, however, is acorns from several species of scrub oaks. Each jay manages to harvest and bury for later use anywhere from six thousand to eight thousand acorns annually. By caching their acorns, scrub jays can eat them throughout the year.

Scrub jays generally forage on or near the ground close to the dense cover of scrub oaks. If one jay finds a particularly large morsel, it will retreat from the rest of the group to eat its prize undisturbed. They are not above stealing food from one another. On many an occasion, I have watched a jay cache an acorn only to have another jay hop over, unearth it, and then fly off to bury it somewhere else.

I settled into the sand to observe the interaction between the jays as they rummaged around in the undergrowth. Their daily conversation seems to consist of low guttural trills and warbles. During territorial displays, females occasionally throw back their heads and belt out a distinctive "hiccup" call. This may be a rallying cry for the males in the family to chase away intruding jays. The sentinel uses distinctive warning calls to alert family members to predators in the area. If an aerial predator is spotted, the sentinel gives an alarm call and all jays dash for dense cover. If the sentinel spies a ground predator such as a snake or bobcat, it gives alarm scolds, and the family group converges to mob the hapless creature.

Florida scrub jays require low-growing scrub oaks and bare sandy patches maintained by periodic burning for feeding and nesting. Woolfenden and Fitzpatrick believe that the Florida scrub jay's complex social system may have evolved as an adaptive response for surviving in fragmented, open scrub habitat. This social structure revolves around a family group that occasionally contains up to eight individuals, but usually averages three or four birds. At the core of the family group is a breeding pair who mate for life and keep a year-round territory. After fledging, their offspring stay in the natal, or birth, territory as "helpers" (much like red-cockaded woodpeckers) for at least a year before attempting to disperse. This is a fundamental characteristic that distinguishes them from scrub jays in western North

Above: *Newly planted orange trees mark the beginning of a citrus grove and the end of another parcel of oak scrub, one of the rarest ecosystems in North America. Scrub is prized for agricultural and urban development because it is dry and well-drained, meaning there is virtually no chance of flooding.*

Left: *Florida scrub jays often post a sentinel to keep watch while the other birds in the family feed. This jay's post is at the top of one of the taller scrub oaks in full flower.*

America. Young jays of the western species leave home as soon as they are independent.

Helpers assist the breeding pair in daily activities such as feeding nestlings and fledglings, defending the territory, performing sentinel duties, and mobbing predators. This assistance, probably born more so from the instinctive motivation to defend their genetic line than from true altruism, increases the chance that the breeding adults will successfully raise offspring. However, helpers do not build nests, incubate eggs, or brood young.

Scrub jays are not the only rare animals in oak scrub, nor is oak scrub the only variety of scrub. I talked with Dr. Eric Menges, a plant ecologist at Archbold Biological Station, to find out more about scrub and its inhabitants, as well as the status of scrub throughout the state. According to Menges, only 5 to 10 percent of the scrub that was present before European settlement remains throughout the state. Some areas have a little bit more, some a little less; many sites are small, and a lot of them are over-grown. Most have not been burned in years, so they are somewhat degraded. Because they are so small and fragmented, there is a lot of "edge" that makes them susceptible to invasion by exotic organisms, such as non-native plants and animals, coming in from developed areas.

Native animals that live in scrub include the Florida mouse, scrub lizard, sand skink (a legless lizard that "swims" through sand), blue-tailed mole skink, and several thousand species of insects, spiders, and millipedes. According to Dr. John Fitzpatrick, former director of Archbold Biological Station, "no fewer than thirty-three species of plants restricted to scrub are listed or under review for listing by state and federal endangered species agencies." All of these plants flourish in what may be some of the poorest and driest soils on Earth. Nineteen plants are found only on the Lake Wales Ridge, including the scrub blazing star, pygmy fringe tree, Carter's mustard, papery whitlow-wort, and wedge-leaf button snakeroot.

To a casual observer, most scrubs look the same because they share many of the same species of plants. According to Menges, there are enough differences to warrant distinguishing four varieties of scrub: oak, sand pine, rosemary (not the spice), and oak-Florida hickory. On many sites, the varieties may grade into each other. For example, sand pine scrub may give way to oak scrub and oak scrub to rosemary. Says Menges, "Rosemary scrub may be the most important as far as conservation is concerned because the majority of plants endemic to scrub are specialists to rosemary scrub. Rosemary scrub is probably the most xeric [dry], and there is a lot of open space. Many of the plants that are specialized to rosemary scrub are very small, herbaceous plants or small woody plants that cannot thrive in a great mass of oak shrubs."

Sand pine scrub is closely related to rosemary scrub (rosemary scrub can have a sand pine canopy). In white sands, there is often a sand pine overstory rising above a rosemary shrub understory. Yellow sands more often have an oak understory beneath a canopy of sand pines. The oak scrub, sometimes called scrubby flatwoods, is quite dense and not as dry as sand pine scrub or rosemary scrub. This scrub is dominated by several oaks, including scrub oak, Chapman's oak, sand live oak, and myrtle oak. Oak scrub grows back much quicker after a fire compared to rosemary scrub, and it also tends not to have as many specialists as rosemary scrub.

There is a fourth scrub that is a variation on oak scrub—oaks mixed with Florida hickory. Oak-Florida hickory scrub grows on yellow sands rather than on the gray sands beneath oak scrub. This is important because there are some small endemic plants that specialize in yellow sand habitat, such

The Lake Placid scrub mint, a rare plant found only in a few sites on the southern Lake Wales Ridge, possesses a chemical compound in its leaves that until recently was unknown to science and had not been previously found anywhere else in nature. This compound interested scientists because of its insecticidal properties and consequent commercial potential as an insect repellent.

as the *Dicerandra* mints. Oak-Florida hickory scrub is not quite as widespread as the other scrubs, and it is floristically similar to sandhill, except that scrubby oaks and hickory dominate rather than longleaf or slash pine.

One aspect of scrub that has always intrigued me has been the different colors of sand. In some areas (particularly oak scrub), the sand is gray, while in others it is brilliant white, a feature that has given rise to a common nickname "sugar sand." Many sites have patches of yellow sand scattered throughout. I was puzzled by this, and I asked Menges what exactly the differences were among these sands other than color? Was it organic content or age? How did the sand affect the vegetation and resulting mix of wildlife to be found in a scrub?

According to Menges, the gray sands of many oak scrubs are closer to the water table than other scrub sands and are not as well-drained. Scrub plants that need slightly moister conditions gravitate toward these areas. Menges and other researchers, however, are not certain how yellow and white sand are different. Some plants are found primarily on white sand while others (such as *Dicerandra* mints) prefer yellow sand—a tendency that baffles researchers. The two soils are similar; there are no significant differences in soil chemistry, organic matter, and soil texture and drainage. Both are low in nutrients, contain little organic matter, and drain rapidly. Yellow sand seems to have a fine clay layer adhering to the grains and is colored by iron in the soil, which is not believed to be important to plant nutrition. However, if a *Dicerandra* mint is planted in white sand, it will grow. Why this doesn't happen in nature is a mystery.

Fire and Scrub

Scrub needs periodic, catastrophic fires that burn virtually everything to the ground in order to maintain its exceptional diversity. Some plants, such as the sand pine, need these hot fires (as opposed to the relatively cool ground fires that sweep through pine forests) to release their seeds. Other plants, such as the scrub oaks, resprout from extensive root systems beneath the soil. Still more plants, including the scrub mints and rosemary, sprout from seeds and flourish in the now open, sun-drenched sand. Most animals escape the flames by retreating to burrows in the sand, such as those of gopher tortoises.

Biologists have long understood that fire is significant in maintaining the diversity of species in scrub, but they have realized only recently that varying the frequency of fires can also be important. Menges says that land managers now understand that there is a natural variation in fire intervals, and if a manager adheres to a rigid schedule for conducting prescribed burns, then he or she is probably not going to promote the diversity of life in that landscape very well—and for good reason. A rigid fire schedule (for example, burning flatwoods every four years) will only benefit the organisms that have adapted to that particular interval between fires. On the other hand, a flexible fire schedule (for example, conducting a series of closely spaced fires followed by longer intervals between fires) would allow plants and animals adapted to either short- or long-term fire intervals to coexist.

When fire is suppressed in scrub for more than fifteen years, sand pines and oaks begin to grow tall and close over open sunlit places in the sand—a process called "canopy closure." As the canopy thickens, small herbaceous and woody plants such as scrub mints are shaded and stop flowering. They do not produce seeds, and slowly die off. After fifteen years without fire, the scrub oaks do not produce as many acorns as they once did, which affects scrub jays and other animals that depend on acorns as a food source. There are fewer scrub animals and plants, and the diversity of scrub organisms on the site decreases dramatically. Menges points to this scenario as an important reason why scrub needs management—you can't just buy it, put a fence around it, and forget it. Otherwise, you'll start to lose the reasons for which it was purchased to protect.

The Importance of Scrub

Florida's scrubs are unique because of the number of endemic plants and animals. One species of particular interest is *Dicerandra frutescens*, the Lake Placid scrub mint, which possesses a chemical compound in its leaves that until recently was unknown to science and had not been previously found anywhere else in nature. This compound interested scientists because of its insecticidal properties and consequent commercial potential as an insect repellent. It was also important from an evolutionary standpoint because it signified that some of these plants could also be unique in their biochemistry.

According to Menges, the *Dicerandra* genus has more than four species that are limited in their range (called "narrow endemics") and grow in different places in Florida. There is one in southern Highlands County, one in northern Highlands County, one near Ocala, and one on the east coast. A fifth species has been discovered near Titusville, and others may soon be described. All of them differ chemically

The hot morning sun burns off the last mist lingering over an oak scrub at Archbold Biological Station. Oak scrub provides important habitat for a multitude of scrub wildlife, including the Florida scrub jay.

American lotus and azola, or mosquito fern, blanket the surface of Lake Kissimmee, one of the largest lakes in Florida. Most central Florida lakes are water-filled sinkholes or flooded depressions that lie between relatively high sandy ridges—the remnants of shorelines that formed thousands of years ago.

in terms of their insecticidal compound. Their leaves and stems look the same, but their flowers are different. Their leaves smell different, too. The mint in northern Highlands county near Sebring is *Dicerandra chrismanii*, a plant said to smell like Vicks Vaporub if you crush a leaf between your fingers. Lake Placid scrub mint occurs on land owned by Archbold Biological Station. Menges believes the *Dicerandra* mints may have separated into different species only within the last few thousand years (perhaps because of the gradual isolation of their arid scrub habitat as the climate changed)—a possibility that excites biogeographers interested in why and how animals and plants speciate.

Lakes

Central Florida is peppered with small lakes, most of them flooded sinkholes or depressions that lie between relatively high sandy ridges—the remnants of shorelines from millennia long past. Many of the larger lakes are part of "chain-of-lakes" systems. Many lakes lack a surface drainage, which means the same water remains in those lakes for a long time, unlike those in more northern states, where new water constantly flows in and older water flows out at a rate of five to ten times faster than in Florida's lakes. In most central Florida lakes, water is released through evaporation or plant transpiration, although water sometimes disappears through sinks connected with the aquifer, particularly during a prolonged drought.

Because these Florida lakes take so long to flush (cycle water through), they are extremely vulnerable to eutrophication—a state in which the level of nutrients such as nitrogen and phosphorus in the water is abnormally high. A eutrophic lake favors the growth of huge blooms of algae, which resemble pea soup, and subsequently results in the death of most life in the lake due to a lack of oxygen as the algae die and inadequate sunlight reaching underwater plants. Leaky septic tanks and farm runoff are two major sources of unneeded nutrients to Florida's lakes.

When Florida's lakes are healthy, they brim with fish, including some forty native species such as largemouth bass, bluegill, black crappie, chain and redfin pickerel, and various catfishes. Lakes provide important breeding habitat for amphibians and feeding and nesting areas for many wading birds, reptiles, and fish. They are essential stopovers for migratory ducks and other waterfowl. Vegetation is generally lush along the water's edge, dominated by bands of herbaceous emergent or floating plants as well as hydrophytic (water-loving) trees and shrubs, including bald cypress, water hickory, water oak, laurel oak, sweetbay, black gum, water elm, Virginia willow, wax myrtle, buttonbush, primrose willow, pickerelweed, arrowhead, American lotus, bladderworts, water lilies, cattail, and bulrush.

Lake levels in Florida naturally fluctuate, typically with the season. During the summer and early fall, water levels are high because of the daily deluges

doing so disrupting the chain of life in lakes. Water hyacinth is thought to have been introduced into the United States from Brazil in 1884 at the Cotton Centennial Exposition in New Orleans. Hydrilla was introduced to Florida by the aquarium trade in the early 1960s and remains the most troublesome aquatic weed in Florida.

Native Dry Prairies

Native dry prairies are nearly as rare as scrub, although good examples of prairie still exist at Myakka River State Park, Three Lakes Wildlife Management Area, and the National Audubon Society's Kissimmee Prairie Sanctuary. Most, however, have been altered for livestock grazing and citrus groves. Brian Millsap, Chief of the Florida Game and Fresh Water Fish Commission's Bureau of Nongame Wildlife, considers dry prairie "one of Florida's most neglected ecosystems."

Dry prairies are also known as "grassland prairies" or "palmetto prairies"; they are not the same as the tallgrass and shortgrass prairies of the Midwest. Dry prairies do not host as many endemic or endangered species as scrub, but there are many notable, fascinating creatures, including the gopher tortoise, eastern diamondback rattlesnake, Florida panther, sandhill crane, and crested caracara, that are becoming increasingly rare with the decline of their natural habitat. The Florida grasshopper sparrow is one of the rarest of dry prairie species, with perhaps only two hundred breeding pairs remaining. Biologists have noticed that the sparrows have been frequenting pastures and fields that are reverting back to prairie—an observation that offers hope that the sparrows will respond to habitat restoration efforts.

The crested caracara has been holding its own despite the conversion of dry prairies to cattle pastures. My first encounter with crested caracaras occurred late one summer afternoon as I drove east on State Road 70, which cuts across the south-central part of Florida from Ft. Pierce to Tampa. I was returning home after a trip to Archbold Biological Station when I noticed a road-killed raccoon off to

from afternoon thundershowers. Lake levels drop from late fall through spring as rainfall decreases. This seasonal fluctuation is critical to maintaining the diversity of plants and animals in the lakes because it forces the zones of plants to move up and down with the water level—creating a positive stress on the ecosystem because no single group of plants is allowed to become dominant. This in turn diversifies the habitat and food available to animals living in and around the lakes.

Humans compromise the health of lakes by artificially maintaining a constant water level throughout the year, eliminating the natural fluctuation. A stabilized lake favors a monoculture of certain species adapted to whatever level water is held at, reducing diversity and the value of the lakeshore habitat to plants and creatures. It also slows down decomposition, allowing muck to accumulate on the lake bottom. Furthermore, humans have introduced exotic aquatic plants, such as the water hyacinth and hydrilla, both considered major pests because they spread rapidly, crowding out native plants and in

Above: *Wiregrass, wildflowers, and saw palmetto turn golden in the early morning sunlight at the National Audubon Society's Ordway-Whittel Kissimmee Prairie Preserve. Native dry prairies are nearly as rare as scrub, although good examples of prairie still exist at this preserve, Myakka River State Park, and Three Lakes Wildlife Management Area.*

Right: *The crested caracara, a dry-prairie species threatened with extinction, is thought by some ornithologists to have derived its name from its harsh, rattling call, in which the head is tilted so that it touches the upper back. "Clyde," the caracara pictured here, is permanently crippled and cannot be returned to the wild. He is used for educational purposes and was photographed in a cattle pasture during a study in central Florida.*

the side of the road. Two caracaras rose from the carcass to perch on nearby fenceposts. The sun's low angle bathed the birds in a warm wash of light that glowed through their spread wings as they landed on the narrow posts. I slowed down and turned my truck around, finally rolling to a stop about two hundred feet away so that I could take a longer look. The birds fidgeted nervously and then flew from the posts, landing about midway across a large pasture. I was without binoculars at the time, so all I could see was two small silhouettes standing in the short grass. They would not return to their meal until I was gone. Disappointed and mentally kicking myself for leaving my binoculars at home, I continued on my way, reflecting on my fleeting encounter with these remarkable members of the falcon family.

The crested caracara is found in only three areas of the United States: south-central Florida, southeastern Texas, and southwestern Arizona. An adult caracara is about twenty-three inches long, slightly larger than what field guides describe as "crow-

sized." The head is large, flattened on top, with an orange, bare-skinned face and a black crown sporting a bushy crest that is erected only when the bird is agitated or threatened. The beak is formidable, shaped much like an eagle's. A distinctive white throat and neck provide striking contrast to the blackish-brown body. The breast and upper back are lightly barred, as is the tail. The caracara's long, sturdy yellow legs and conspicuous white wing patches, visible near the wing tips when the bird is in flight, make it unmistakable, even when viewed from a distance. Caracaras are known for their distinctive, harsh, rattling cry—thought by some ornithologists to be the origin of their name—during which the head is thrown so far back that it touches the upper back.

In Florida, the crested caracara is listed as a threatened species by state and federal governments, meaning that it is in danger of serious decline. The birds keep year-round territories and do not migrate. Caracaras have been surviving on ranches because the cattle keep the grass cropped short, a modification to the caracara's native habitat that the birds don't seem to mind because they can walk around easily while searching for food. The caracaras nest almost exclusively in cabbage palms. Ranchers generally do not destroy these trees because they provide shade for cattle.

The problem for the caracaras, however, is that the open pastures of cattle ranches, like the native dry prairies they replaced, are disappearing all too quickly. Ranch land is being converted to citrus groves or being paved over to make way for trailer parks, shopping centers, and other urban development. Unless measures are taken to curtail this trend, there is little hope the birds will be able to sustain their numbers over time.

Joan Morrison, a biologist with the Department of Wildlife Ecology and Conservation at the University of Florida, should know. She and her team have been in the field almost continuously over the last few years studying these threatened birds. The purpose of her work has been to study the ecology of crested caracaras, evaluate the status of the Florida population, and provide data that can be used to develop management plans for helping the birds survive. To do this, the team has been capturing adults and fledglings and fitting them with radio transmitters. Once fitted, the caracaras are released, and Morrison follows their movements over several months by tracking signals from the transmitters by plane. Data gathered from the movements of adult caracaras can be used to determine the size of territories, which include the areas they use for feeding and nesting. Data obtained by following the movements of immature caracaras may provide important information regarding the young birds' use of habitat, their ability to survive their nomadic first few years, and finally, where they wander as they seek their own territories.

Morrison's findings—although preliminary and focused on Florida's population of crested caracaras—offer considerable insight into little-known aspects of the ecology of the species in general. According to Morrison, crested caracaras are social and form strong pair bonds. They set up permanent territories that frequently overlap those of neighboring pairs, at least in feeding areas. Caracaras may range as far as two miles from their nests to find food, yet the nests may be surprisingly close together—as near as a half-mile on some large ranches with lots of good habitat. Furthermore, crested caracaras spend much more time foraging in wetlands than people realize. "We are finding a lot of wetland-dependent creatures in the food they are bringing in, particularly around nesting time," said Morrison. "These animals include cotton rats, marsh rabbits, fish, amphibians, and snakes." Information such as this is crucial not only because it indicates the importance of wetlands to caracaras, but it underlines the continued need to preserve wetland areas, particularly around ranches.

Morrison's observations also add more weight to the growing body of evidence that crested caracaras are less scavengers than opportunistic generalists, willing and able to eat almost anything they can find. Fish, birds, small mammals, turtles, amphibians, invertebrates, carrion—all of these items find their way down the nondiscriminating gullets of caracaras. The ability to take advantage of a diverse array of foods is a useful trait that may help the birds survive vagaries in prey populations or environmental conditions.

In spite of the tenuous situation of crested caracara populations in North America, little research has been conducted on their behalf. No one is sure how many caracaras are left in the wild. Joan Morrison's research in Florida suggests that mosaics of open, grassy prairies, wetlands, and hammocks must be preserved in order for the birds to survive. But how much territory do they need? How do young birds find new territories? How old must caracaras be before they can breed? How long do they live? Until we devote the time and resources to answer these questions and the many more that have yet to be asked, the future of these exquisite raptors, as well as that of everything wild in an increasingly developed central Florida, is uncertain.

Above: *Sandhill cranes frequent both dry prairies and marshes in central Florida. This adult and chick were foraging for insects and frogs in a marsh at Myakka River State Park.*
Left: *An ancient bald cypress and rocks loom as river smoke rises from the rapids of the Hillsborough River on a cold spring morning at Hillsborough River State Park.*

Chapter 6

South Florida

Mahogany Hammock, one of the largest tropical hardwood hammocks remaining in Everglades National Park, is also among the most beautiful. On this spring morning, the air in the hammock is cool and humid and pungent with the smell of wet, tropical vegetation. High clouds, remnants from last night's rain, blanket the sun like thin gauze, diffusing the light washing over the hammock canopy, rendering every shard of bark and leaf in exquisite detail. As I walk along the boardwalk that threads through the heart of the hammock, a blue-gray gnatcatcher drops to a branch no more than three feet from my face, twittering to itself. It is a delicate little bird, barely three inches long, with a quick eye, white eye ring, and muted plumage. A barred owl hoots from a nearby tree, invisible against the green and brown tapestry of canopy. I can't see him, but I know he is watching. A red-shouldered hawk screams overhead and the gnatcatcher vanishes.

Facing page: *White ibis and anhingas flock to their roosts near sunset at the A. R. Marshall Loxahatchee National Wildlife Refuge in the northern Everglades, just south of the Palm Beaches.*
Above: *A baby alligator sleeps soundly in the sun at Fakahatchee Strand, knowing its mother is keeping watch only a few feet away. The flower is a yellow bladderwort, a carnivorous plant that traps small insects and minnows in its underwater bladders.*

As I walk deeper into the hammock, the musky, sweet smell of white stopper pervades the air. Sometimes the smell grows sweeter, as if there is a secret flower blooming among the leaves. Trees loom over the boardwalk—pigeon plum, poisonwood, strangler fig, wild tamarind, royal palms, gumbo limbo, and mahogany. Other trees beyond the boardwalk lean sharply or have been toppled completely, testimony to the power of hurricane winds. The air is liquid and luminous; thick, tropical leaves droop and shed songbirds like bright raindrops.

A torrent of bird song rushes and eddies through the hammock; most likely it is a Carolina wren. Long, green anoles (a type of lizard) slink along the rails of the boardwalk, occasionally flashing the red fold of skin under the throat at the sight of another male or a female. In the leaf litter and low plants beneath the boardwalk creep countless insects, spiders, skinks (another type of lizard), frogs, and an occasional rattlesnake. Much of the life in the hammock is hidden, finding refuge from heat, wind, or prying eyes. The hammock itself is a sanctuary for anything that cannot survive in the bright, exposed, often sodden expanse of saw grass that surrounds it.

Near noon, toward the end of my walk through the hammock, the sun emerges. As I leave the hammock and cross the section of boardwalk that leads back to the parking lot, I am pummeled by the heat and blinding light of midday. Billowing clouds march across the sky, darkening the saw grass with their advance and brightening them with their passage. A cloud covers the sun, and I feel a breath of cool air and the spatter of rain. It has been a morning well spent.

The Defining Force of Water

Mahogany Hammock is but a speck of forest in the more than one and a half million acres that is Everglades National Park. Much of south Florida's natural landscape of cypress swamps, marshes, hardwood

Another south Florida day comes to a close as the sun slips below the horizon of Florida Bay, East Cape Sable, Everglades National Park.

hammocks, pine forests, and mangrove swamps, including many portions of Big Cypress Swamp and Florida Bay, has been preserved in federal, state, and privately owned parks as well. These wild areas, however, are bounded by extensive urban sprawl, including the corridor of concrete that extends from West Palm Beach south through Miami on the Atlantic Coast and Fort Myers and Naples on the Gulf Coast.

The cities are thirsty, needing water for drinking, irrigation, and play. Millions of gallons of fresh water are pumped out of the Biscayne Aquifer each day to supply their demand, with sad consequences for the surrounding environment, including the disappearance of the quiet springs that once bubbled up through the limestone near the Everglades and in Biscayne Bay, south of Miami. The historic headwaters of the Everglades—Lake Okeechobee and the chain of lakes that feed into the Kissimmee River—have been altered to stabilize their natural, seasonal fluctuations of water level to satisfy human needs, to the detriment of the wildlife and natural communities in and around the lakes.

To provide flood control for cities near Lake Okeechobee, engineers constructed levees around the perimeter of the lake, which historically flooded its banks and spilled south into the Everglades. The meandering Kissimmee River was straightened into a deep, straight canal dubbed "the Ditch" by disapproving south Florida environmentalists. Marshes dried up and water quality in Lake Okeechobee deteriorated rapidly with the influx of sewage and runoff from fields that no longer were purified by flowing slowly through the marshes. Levees and more than 1,400 miles of canals for irrigation and flood control have splintered the landscape, shunting water from areas that desperately need it and flooding others.

Water is the defining force of many south Florida ecosystems, and a number of landscapes have been altered dramatically as a result of changes to the amount and quality of water they receive. Ranches now surround much of the north and west sides of Lake Okeechobee, while agribusinesses (primarily sugar cane) cover almost all of the deep peat soil east and particularly south of the lake, where once there was a magnificent custard (pond) apple swamp. Marjory Stoneman Douglas described this swamp in her classic 1947 book, *The Everglades: River of Grass,* as a place where custard apple trees "grew fiercely . . . edged with tall leather ferns and Boston ferns and knotted with vines, which no man could get through without axes or dynamite." Populations of wading birds have dwindled by as much as 90 percent, and many other magnificent creatures are close to extinction or have disappeared completely.

In 1883, reporter A. P. Williams, a member of an expedition sent by the New Orleans *Times-Democrat* newspaper to explore south Florida, commented after traversing the Everglades from Lake Okeechobee to the Gulf of Mexico in a small boat, "They [the Everglades] are nothing more or less than a vast and useless marsh, and such they will remain for all time to come, in all probability." Today, Everglades National Park and Big Cypress National Preserve protect only about one-fifth of the original Everglades. Much has changed in little more than one hundred years.

Florida Bay

Florida Bay lies between the southern tip of Florida and the Keys. It covers more than eight hundred and fifty square miles, of which more than 80 percent falls within the borders of Everglades National Park. It is a sundrenched, subtropical estuary, born of the meeting between fresh water and salt water, stippled by more than two hundred tiny, mangrove-rimmed keys (islands). In some areas, the water is startlingly clear, while in others it is the color of the slick, gray, mudlike marl that covers the bottom.

The bay is home to American crocodiles, bottlenose dolphins, West Indian manatees, sea turtles, several species of wading birds, ospreys, bald eagles, and brown pelicans. Beds of seagrass wave in clear water, which over much of the bay averages only about five feet deep—shallow enough to walk across. Speckled sea trout, redfish, tarpon, barracuda,

sharks, and rays move through the bay and its seagrass beds and tangle of submerged mangrove roots edging the islands. The waters of Florida Bay are the principal inshore nursery for Tortugas pink shrimp and provide important habitat for spiny lobster and stone crab. Southwestern Florida Bay is noted for its hardbottom habitats that support sponges and hard and soft coral communities.

Although the limestone bedrock beneath Florida Bay is quite flat, the muddy bottom is not. Peat and mud have accumulated over the last 4,500 years to form a series of intertidal mud banks and mangrove islands that dissect the bay into shallow basins known locally as "lakes." This underwater landscape is not static; sediments are constantly being deposited and carried away, resulting in shifts in the mud banks and islands that "migrate."

Florida Bay requires a constant mixing of fresh and salt water to remain healthy. Tidal action and longshore currents mix bay water with that of the Gulf of Mexico. There is also an interchange of water with the Straits of Florida through several channels between islands in the Keys. Fresh water flows into Florida Bay primarily through Taylor Slough and numerous small creeks. The bay also receives fresh water from Shark River Slough, but only after it has mixed with salt water from the Gulf of Mexico and flowed east around Cape Sable at Florida's southernmost tip. The headwaters of both of these sloughs lie in managed or developed areas outside of Everglades National Park; as a result, much of the water is diverted away from Florida Bay. Scientists believe the bay also receives some of its fresh water through groundwater seepage from the peninsula. Salinity varies widely in Florida Bay due to water management practice and ranges from brackish to nearly twice that of sea water. The salinity may vary seasonally as well, with the lowest salinity generally recorded from July through October because of the deluge of fresh water dumped on the bay and Everglades during heavy afternoon thunderstorms.

The health of Florida Bay began to decline in 1987 with the die-off of thousands of acres of seagrass. Decaying plant matter increased the turbidity of the water and created conditions favorable for large and persistent blooms of algae that continue to this day. The die-off is also believed to have contributed to the death of sponges near the Florida Keys and a decline of commercial and sport fisheries. Over the past thirty years, water managers have diverted storm water that would have otherwise reached Florida Bay, and fewer hurricanes have hit south Florida than normal when compared to the historical record. Higher salinity in many parts of the bay because of less fresh water, combined with elevated water temperature over a period of several years, may have been what caused the seagrass to die.

I have hope that conditions will begin to improve in Florida Bay. Water managers are now required to allow more fresh water to flow through the Everglades and into the bay. Seagrass beds are gradually recovering. The National Park Service and eight other agencies have formed an Interagency Program Management Committee to coordinate research activities and ensure that a comprehensive effort is maintained until Florida Bay is restored as a healthy, integrated component of the entire south Florida ecosystem.

Freshwater Marshes

No finer words have been written to describe the unique character of the Everglades than this description by Marjory Stoneman Douglas from *The Everglades: River of Grass*:

> There are no other Everglades in the world. They are, they have always been, one of the unique regions of the earth, remote, never wholly known. Nothing anywhere else is like them: their vast glittering openness, wider than the enormous visible round of the horizon, the racing free saltness and sweetness of their massive winds, under the dazzling blue heights of space. They are unique also in the simplicity, the diversity, the related harmony of the forms of life they enclose. The miracle of the light pours over the green and brown expanse of saw grass and of water, shining and slow-moving below, the grass and the water that is the meaning and the central fact of the Everglades of Florida. It is a river of grass.

The Everglades are synonymous with Florida, attracting millions of visitors from around the world each year. Much of it is saw grass marsh, within which herons and egrets are sometimes seen feed-

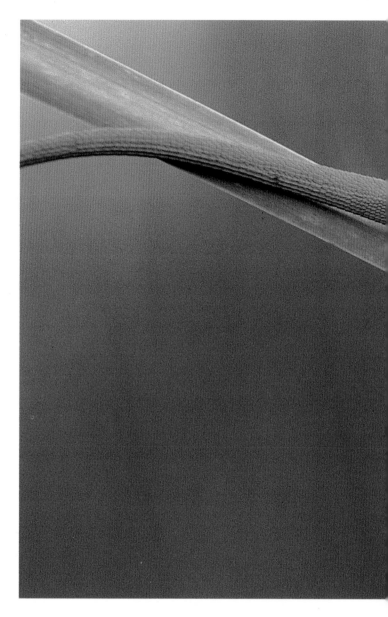

ing in the hundreds among the tall blades. Where the saw grass merges with cypress prairie, red-shouldered hawks sit and survey a kingdom of sun and clouds and sedge.

Approximately 70 percent of the remaining Everglades landscape is covered with saw grass, which is actually a sedge and not a true grass. To understand why saw grass got its name, rub your fingers gently along an edge. Each blade is edged with tiny, sharp teeth, like a saw. In the central Everglades, the saw grass is impressive; the plants stand more than ten feet tall and form a virtually impenetrable mass that extends beyond the horizon. When viewed from the air, dark green hammocks occasionally break the continuum of saw grass like the shadows of clouds.

Above: *A green anole extends its strawberry-colored dewlap while perched on a saw grass blade at the A. R. Marshall Loxahatchee National Wildlife Refuge.*

Left: *Strangler figs are capable of growing as free-standing trees, but most often they sprout as seeds high in another tree, send tendril roots down toward the ground, and then wrap around their unfortunate host. Although strangler figs are not parasitic, the host tree often dies, shaded out by the fig. This strangler fig has wrapped around a mahogany at Mahogany Hammock, Everglades National Park.*

Above: *A red-shouldered hawk scans its surroundings for prey while perched in a buttonwood tree at Everglades National Park.* Right: *Cumulus clouds develop above a group of mangrove islands on a still morning in Florida Bay. Florida Bay covers more than 850 square miles, of which more than 80 percent falls within the borders of Everglades National Park. It requires a constant mixing of fresh and salt water to remain healthy. Because much of the fresh water that normally flows into Florida Bay has been diverted to urban and agricultural areas, salinity varies widely, ranging from brackish to nearly twice that of sea water. The lack of fresh water entering the bay is believed to be a major factor in its decline, which includes a die-off of thousands of acres of seagrass and large, persistent blooms of algae.*

Saw grass covers many areas of Big Cypress Swamp as well, but here I see more of a diversity of types of marsh than in most areas of the Everglades. Wet prairies and flag marshes grade into or are imbedded in expanses of saw grass and cordgrass. Of the marsh systems, wet prairies are flooded for the least amount of time—only fifty to one hundred and fifty days per year. Because of this shorter hydroperiod, they are considered the most species-rich of Florida's marshes and include many varieties of grasses, sedges, and wildflowers. The plants in these wet prairies are of much shorter stature than in saw grass marshes. Flag marshes occur in pockets of slightly deeper water and are named after pick-

erelweed, fire flag, arrowhead, and other wetland plants with flaglike leaves.

Marsh plants in south Florida are well adapted to seasons of flood and drought. Most marsh plants, including saw grass, propagate vegetatively, meaning they expand from existing roots and stems. Few plants apart from truly aquatic (submerged) species can germinate or survive as seedlings when submerged. Seeds germinate from seed banks in the marsh substrate only if the surface water has completely disappeared during the dry season. The dry season also allows nutrients tied up in dead vegetation and detritus to be released back into the soil, initiating a growth spurt in surrounding plants. Plants such as saw grass and cordgrass living in south Florida marshes have evolved in a system with low nutrient levels. If nutrient levels increase dramatically, such as is the case when farm runoff is allowed to flow through saw grass marshes, cattails tend to crowd out the other species and the delicate, interdependent web of life in the marshes is thrown out of balance.

Fires are frequent in Everglades marshes and have been for thousands of years. In fact, it is charcoal from ancient fires that has colored the peat beneath the marshes a rich black. Marsh plants are well adapted to fire. Saw grass, pickerelweed, arrowhead, and maidencane quickly grow again following fire because of the bound-up nutrients released into the soil by burning plant matter and the reduced competition for space. Saw grass, in particular, is adapted to frequent fire. Saw grass blades are so flammable that they can carry a fire over standing water. The growing bud is covered by soil and insulated by overlapping leaves to protect it from fire.

After a fire, saw grass grows quickly, reaching a height of nearly fourteen inches in two weeks. This rapid regrowth allows the plant to outpace rising water levels associated with early summer thunderstorms (when lightning is most frequent), which would kill the stem if it was completely submerged. If a marsh does not burn for a long time, the intense heat from a fire burning through accumulated dead organic material can scorch the soil and kill the saw grass, eliminating the toothy sedge from that area.

In many areas of the Everglades, broad shallow channels called sloughs (pronounced "slews") meander through the marshes. The deeper sloughs, which are often aligned with linear depressions in the underlying limestone bedrock, have water flow throughout the year, except during extreme drought. Pond apple, pop ash, fragrant water lily, and other floating aquatic plants are common. Toward the end of the dry season, sloughs and alligator holes may hold the only water to be found for miles around.

Cypress Strands

In Big Cypress Swamp, sloughs flow through linear forests of cypress called strands. Among the largest and most beautiful strands are Fakahatchee, Roberts Lake, Deep Lake, and Gator Hook. The strands are dominated by bald cypress, red maple, laurel oak, cabbage palm, strangler fig, red bay, sweet bay, wax myrtle, and leather fern, among others. In Fakahatchee Strand, native Florida royal palms occur. The canopy trees of the strands are generally temperate species, while plants in the understory are mainly tropical.

Sometimes small strands of pond cypress form along short, shallow depressions in the limestone bedrock. On a late afternoon in September, I hiked

Male and female snail kites clash over perching rights near a nest in Conservation Area 2A in Broward County. The snail kite is an endangered species that feeds almost exclusively on apple snails, freshwater snails common throughout much of Florida. The talons of snail kites are longer and thinner than most other raptors for plucking snails from the water, while the beak is sharply hooked for pulling the body of the snail from its shell.

Left, top: *Puffy cumulus clouds reflect on the calm open waters of Lake Okeechobee. Lake Okeechobee is the largest lake in Florida and the second largest lake in the continental United States, yet it is less than seventeen feet deep.*

Left, bottom: *The setting sun blazes through parting storm clouds on the Wild and Scenic Loxahatchee River at Jonathan Dickinson State Park. The skeleton trees on the right are cypress that died when salt water moved up the river after Jupiter Inlet was modified into a permanent inlet. Red mangroves have become established over much of the Lower Loxahatchee River.*

into such a strand off Turner River Road in Big Cypress National Preserve. Carrying a hip pack of 35mm camera gear and a waterproof backpack filled with equipment for my 4x5 camera, I tried to cover the half mile to the cypress strand before the warm afternoon light faded. Three great blue herons flew overhead, tossing single squawks among each other, perhaps to maintain formation or pursue some means of heron communication known only to them. I was following a swamp buggy trail, which provided a faster track to the strand than blazing my own trail through thigh-high cordgrass. Midway between the strand and the road, I passed through a narrow pineland that had burned recently; green spikes of grass and palmetto poked through the charred earth and limestone.

As I neared the strand, the water got deeper and the mud thicker. I tried desperately not to pitch forward on my face or sink into mud above my boots. For every step I took, I sunk three or four inches. Sometimes the mud would grasp; other times I was released without a struggle. I passed hundreds of crayfish mounds, each with a hole in the top, like a miniature volcano.

Finally, I reached the strand and looked around for the best angle to emphasize the wide cypress buttresses. The sun was nearing the horizon, but the portion of cypress trunk facing the west was still warmed by the light. I raced through my Polaroids to check my exposure and composition, and then inserted holders of transparency film. After the third transparency, the warm light winked out, fading to dull peach and then to purple within a couple of minutes. The sun had set. As I packed up my gear, the surrounding saw grass and cypress grew increasingly blue, and light washed the high cirrus clouds overhead like a delicate dye through lamb's fleece. Barred owls called "who-cooks-for-you, who-cooks-for-you-all" from a large strand in the distance. As daylight creatures headed to their homes, those who roamed the night began their activities.

The Florida Panther

One animal active primarily at night, at least during the hot summer months, is the Florida panther.

Remnants of the day's storms set a dramatic backdrop to a dwarf cypress prairie in Everglades National Park.

The range of the Florida panther is believed to have once covered Florida, Georgia, Mississippi, Louisiana, South Carolina, and parts of Tennessee, merging with the Texas puma to the west, the Rocky Mountain puma to the northwest in Arkansas and Missouri, and the eastern mountain lion (now thought to be extinct) to the north. Now the Florida panther has been reduced to a core population of thirty to fifty cats in southwest Florida, and to rumors in other areas of Florida. Before European settlement, ecologists estimate there may have been more than 1,300 panthers in Florida alone. Panthers and humans conflicted as settlers cut down the forests and expanded towns and settlements. Settlers feared for their livestock, their game, and their lives, and duly set out to extirpate the big cats. They were largely successful.

Florida panthers are smaller than most other North American cougars, ranging in weight from eighty to one hundred and fifty pounds and measuring more than seven feet in length. They are tawny and relatively dark reddish-gray on top and light gray on the undersides. There are no black Florida panthers. Adult panthers require a home range ranging from one hundred to four hundred square miles, preferring drier upland areas of hammocks and pinelands imbedded within swamps and marshes for hunting their primary large quarries—whitetailed deer and wild hogs. Panthers kill their prey by biting through the vertebrae in the neck or through the back of the skull.

The territories of female panthers often overlap with those of a male. Females space themselves according to how much prey is available, while males try to incorporate as many females into their home range as possible. Because male panthers play no role in raising kittens and females may come into heat any time of year, a male panther can increase his chances of siring offspring by regularly checking the reproductive status of females whose territories are included within his own.

Adult panthers are generally solitary animals and

Morning sun illuminates the fog in a pine rocklands in Everglades National Park. Much of this forest was destroyed when Hurricane Andrew swept through on August 24, 1992.

usually associate with each other only to mate. The act of mating is often violent, involving snarling, cuffing, and biting (a trait universal among cats), and the cats may mate several times a day.

Kittens are born about three months after conception, usually from March through July in a den hidden in the saw palmettos. Each kitten weighs about a pound and is eight to twelve inches in length, with tawny fur dappled with black spots on the body and black bands on the tail. The eyes are blue at birth and turn amber as the kittens mature. Panther kittens are most vulnerable during their first six months, which is when they are most likely to meet with accidents or fall prey to predators, including male panthers. After being weaned at about two months, kittens learn to hunt from their mother, sharing her kills and staying with her for up to eighteen months.

Although Florida panthers are now protected as an endangered subspecies, they are faced with a host of insidious, potentially lethal problems, including low genetic variability (sons are breeding with mothers, brothers with sisters, and so on), males with only one testicle and a high percentage of defective sperm, and kittens with heart murmurs. High levels of mercury have been found in fish, raccoons, and other animals in south Florida, and at least one panther has died as a result of mercury poisoning. Diminishing habitat has crowded panthers into smaller ranges, causing territorial fights that have resulted in the deaths of several cats.

Panthers are not alone in their struggle for survival in south Florida. Virtually every wild creature faces the predicament of how to make do with less habitat. As south Florida's human population expands, so does its demands on water, land, and clean air. Orange groves and vegetable farms creep down from the north, and cities push in from the east and west. Wildlife is too often considered expendable—the price of progress. We must realize that humans and wildlife are partners in the same furious dance of life. Without these partners, we dance alone.

Above: *A Florida panther peers down from an oak limb in the Fakahatchee Strand. This Florida panther is one of less than fifty remaining in the wild. Florida panthers enjoy complete protection under the Endangered Species Act, but suffer from low genetic variability and insufficient remaining habitat—both significant problems contributing to the panthers' already uncertain future. (Photo © Dave Maehr)*

Right: *The last rays of the setting sun glow on the rough bark and wide buttresses of pond cypress in Big Cypress National Preserve.*

Chapter 7

The Atlantic Coast

"Always the edge of the sea remains an elusive and undefinable boundary," wrote Rachel Carson in her classic book from 1955, *The Edge of the Sea*. The tide washes in and then recedes, leaving the shoreline changed with each passing. Waves hammer at sand and rock, bringing forth material for a new shoreline configuration and taking away the remnants of the old. Even the level of the ocean itself is constantly shifting; sea level has risen and fallen at least thirty times over the last three million years, establishing an approximately 100,000-year cycle of inundation and regression. The effects of this activity leave indelible marks in the geological record and read like chapters in Earth's diary, within which Florida's Atlantic Coast is an elegant entry.

Facing page: *A great blue heron greets the morning from atop a beach piling at Canaveral National Seashore.*
Above: *A winter storm approaches over a salt marsh tidal creek at Big Talbot Island State Park.*

My vantage of the Atlantic Ocean on this October evening is afforded from a camp on the beach at the north end of Canaveral National Seashore. A steady wind from the east keeps sandflies and mosquitoes back up in the vegetation on the dunes behind me. An hour ago, an immense pink moon rose from the water and climbed into the darkening sky, growing paler and smaller over the course of its ascent. Now it floats high above the horizon, its mirror image shattered over the tops of waves crashing onto shore. Canaveral National Seashore is one of the few places in Florida where you can camp on a wild, unspoiled beach and gaze out on a scene that is both timeless and precious. It is a place to renew your connection with the Earth, measure the passage of time by the ebb and flow of the tide and by the rising of the sun each new day.

Beach bean is a common plant on Atlantic Coast dunes.

In Florida, the Atlantic coast stretches from the Georgia state line just above Jacksonville south through the Keys. Much of it is "high-energy" coastline, meaning that the wind almost always blows from the ocean toward the land. This steady breeze creates constant wave action, which plays a greater role in sculpting the shoreline than does the offshore breeze and gently lapping "low-energy" waves typical of the mangrove-fringed shores of southwest Florida and the salt marshes of the Nature Coast.

As with high-energy areas of shoreline on the Gulf Coast, Florida's Atlantic coast is flanked by chains of long, narrow, low islands dominated by high dunes. These islands run parallel to the coast and are called barrier islands because they form the mainland shoreline's first line of defense against the fierce wave energy of severe storms and hurricanes. The barrier islands typically consist of beaches and dunes on the ocean side, tidal marshes on the landward side, and lagoons or estuaries separating them from the mainland. The island chains are interrupted by inlets that connect the estuary or lagoon with the open ocean. My campsite at Canaveral National Seashore is on such a barrier island, separated from the mainland by Mosquito Lagoon at the north end of the Indian River Lagoon.

Some of the most pristine barrier islands remaining on the Atlantic Coast include Amelia and Little Talbot Islands north of Jacksonville; Canaveral National Seashore in central Florida; and the portions of Jupiter Island occupied by Hobe Sound National Wildlife Refuge and The Nature Conservancy's Blowing Rocks Preserve. Most of these islands were created over a period of several hundred thousand years by prevailing wind energy combined with sand brought south by the longshore current, or littoral drift. This river of sand, as it is sometimes called, runs parallel to the shore from north to south and deposits sand that originated as sediment washed down from mountain creeks high in the Appalachian Mountains. Much of the sand is pushed toward the shore by waves, where it begins to accumulate. Time passes and a sandbar forms. More sand accumulates, and eventually the sandbar grows to the point where it rises above sea level to create a barrier island.

The original sandy layers deposited before and during the Pamlico Period have fused into a limestone base that underlies these barrier islands. Rock outcroppings of some of this limestone can be seen on the beach at Anastasia State Recreation Area and Blowing Rocks Preserve. The two northernmost Atlantic barriers in Florida, Amelia and Little Talbot Islands, are the southernmost of the sea islands, a chain of barriers extending from South Carolina to Florida. These islands are short and broad, in contrast to the long narrow shape of most Atlantic barriers, and their Recent Epoch sands are often welded onto older Pleistocene barriers.

Dunes

As sand is pushed up on the beach, it begins to dry out. The wind blows the dry sand grains landward in a rolling movement called "saltation." The rolling sand grains stop when they bump into debris or vegetation that has become established on the stable portion of the beach. As the sand accumulates, it forms a dune. Dune vegetation plays a crucial role in maintaining the dune and allowing it to build by catching and holding sand grains with stems, leaves, and extensive root systems. Plant species living on the dune are adapted to survive the constant wind, heat, and high salinity levels found in the constantly shifting conditions of the dune ecosystem. Many of these plants have developed thick, waxy leaves and hairy stems, which help them retain water and keep salt out. Other plants can actually excrete salt or detoxify themselves when salt concentrations become too high. Extensive root systems absorb water quickly and efficiently.

A healthy dune has three distinct zones of plant life occupying different portions of the dune. I am camped on the seaward edge of the dune, down slightly from the low-lying vines and grasses that form the pioneer zone or upper beach and foredune zone. The harshest conditions of the dune exist here, where plant life must survive repeated burials under sand and, occasionally, waves due to rough seas or abnormally high tides. These plants spread out from the dune to the beach, catching and consolidating sand and returning nutrients to the soil that will benefit vegetation in the zones farther back on the dune. The common pioneer species found closest to the beach include railroad vine, silver-leaf croton, and beach bean, with sea oats, beach cordgrass, and bitter panicum occupying the angle up the dune.

Behind these pioneering plants lies the scrub or "prickly" zone, as it is known on the southeast coast; the scrub zone is comprised of a combination of low woody plants, cacti, and succulents. In this zone, sea grapes, inkberry, saw palmetto, Spanish bayonet, and prickly pear cactus are abundant. On beaches along the northeast coast, saw palmetto, dwarfed cabbage palm, and various shrubs and grasses dominate this zone, known also as the transitional zone. These plants occupy the top and upper back area of the dune before grading into the third zone of dune vegetation, known as the forested zone, or, as many botanists consider it, the inland extension of the transitional zone. In the northern half of Florida, saw palmetto, dwarfed cabbage palms, live oak, red bay, magnolia, and wild olive are found in this zone. Salt spray kills the terminal buds of many of these trees, particularly the taller live oaks, thereby producing the "pruned," upwardly sloping canopies that are characteristic of Atlantic coastal hammocks.

In the southern half of the state, pine/palmetto woodlands or tropical hammocks of gumbo limbo, sea grape, and live oak gradually melt into the mangroves and tidal marshes found on the lagoon side of the barrier island. From Cape Canaveral southward, West Indian shrubs, such as Simpson's stopper, naked wood, and white indigoberry, intermix with temperate shrubs and finally replace them in southeast Florida. The vegetation of the dunes behind my campsite and of the maritime forest bordering the lagoon is incredibly diverse because of the mix of tropical and temperate species.

There are a number of human-induced and natural factors that have serious effects on dune and beach ecosystems. Development on the dune was once a tremendous problem; however, federal and state regulations now protect dunes, establishing set-back lines that prevent development within a certain distance from the beach and prohibiting the destruction of dune plants. Although some beachfront developers, property managers, and homeowners still attempt to pave over or cut back dune vegetation to provide easy access to the beach and protect their ocean view, these attempts are often thwarted by environmental groups, government agencies, or neighboring property owners who will sue to ensure that the safety of the dune that protects their property is not threatened.

Exotics, such as Australian pine and California scaveola, can disrupt dune systems by squeezing out native plants, forming monocultures that eliminate much of the diversity of life on the dune. Australian pines are especially damaging since their fallen needles form a dense ground mat that prohibits other plants from growing beneath them. This ultimately reduces the stability of the dune by removing many beneficial native plants that accumulate sand and hold the dune together with their root systems. Fortunately, many communities and nature preserves have begun removing Australian pines and replanting their dunes with native vegetation, which protects the dune, benefits wildlife, and restores the historic beauty of the beach.

Wave action probably has the most serious impact on the stability of the beach and dune systems on barrier islands. Although waves push ashore much needed sand for building the beach and dune, they also erode much of it away and deposit it offshore or on shorelines farther down the coast. Heavy surf caused by northeast storms and hurricanes hastens this process considerably.

While the building and erosion process of the shoreline is nothing new, scientists have noted a shift from a pattern of gradual accumulation to one of gradual erosion. This may be due in part to an increasingly rapid rise in sea level, as well as man-made impacts resulting from attempts to stabilize inlets and the barrier islands' naturally shifting beaches. Such concerns disturb beachfront developers and homeowners, but are far from my mind as the rush and retreat of the surf lulls me to sleep.

Wildlife of the Barrier Islands

Barrier islands and their associated lagoons and estuaries sustain an amazingly diverse assortment of animal life. Many crustaceans and fish, including commercially important shrimp and crabs, as well as sport fish such as snook, snapper, redfish, and sea trout, depend on the estuarine mangrove and tidal marsh areas for their survival. The forested areas of many islands once hosted wildlife such as black bear and Florida panther, in addition to the gray fox, raccoon, and opossum that can still be found today. Barrier island beaches and dunes offer important habitat for burrowing ghost crabs, as well as nesting and feeding areas for many shorebirds. The only place to find Florida's endangered beach mice is among vegetation growing on dunes.

Three species of sea turtles also nest on Florida's Atlantic Coast beaches: loggerhead, green, and leatherback. The loggerhead relies on Florida beaches more so than other species. Some twenty-five thousand loggerhead females nest in the southeastern United States each year from May through early August; as many as fourteen thousand nests are deposited on the stretch of coastline between the inlet at Cape Canaveral south to Sebastian inlet alone. The loggerhead sea turtle is named for the size of its head, which is quite large in proportion to the rest of its body. As sea turtles go, it is a relatively big animal, weighing in at two hundred to three hundred pounds and measuring thirty-three to forty inches in carapace length.

The turtle's broad head contains powerful jaw muscles that enable it to crack or bite off the heavy-shelled clams, crustaceans, and encrusting animals that make up much of its diet. After a female loggerhead crawls up a sandy beach to dig a deep, flask-shaped nest, she lays about one hundred and twenty leathery, ping-pong-ball-sized eggs, which will hatch in about two months. Although the turtle hatchlings emerge at night to evade predators, fewer than one in every thousand survives to maturity.

Many people expect to see dolphins and perhaps an occasional pod of pilot whales off the Atlantic coast of Florida, but they do not anticipate the sight of large whales, such as the northern right whales that bear their calves during the winter in coastal waters from Georgia to northern Florida. Northern right whales are among the rarest of the great whales, with an estimated three hundred and fifty individuals surviving in the North Atlantic Ocean—a stable number perhaps, but hardly increasing despite many decades of protection

Commercial whalers hunted them nearly to extinction during the late 1800s and early 1900s for their oil and baleen, a hornlike substance that grows vertically from the jaws to form a sieve through which they filter zooplankton from seawater. The oil was used for fuel and light, and the baleen, which is flexible like plastic, was incorporated into such items as women's corsets. Right whales were so named by whalers because they were relatively slow-moving, the quality of their oil and baleen was excellent, and they floated when dead—all factors that made them the "right" whales to kill. Northern right whales are now considered an endangered species and protected from hunting by the Marine Mammal Protection Act and the Endangered Species Act. The calving grounds off Georgia and northern

Above: *The loggerhead sea turtle is named for the size of its head, which is quite large in proportion to the rest of its body. As many as fourteen thousand nests are deposited on the stretch of Atlantic coastline between the inlet at Cape Canaveral south to Sebastian inlet, making it possibly the most important nesting area for loggerhead sea turtles in the world. (Photo © Doug Perrine)*

Left: *Coquina limestone formations litter the sand at Washington Oaks State Gardens, creating one of the most interesting beaches on Florida's Atlantic Coast.*

Above: *A reddish egret is mirrored in a salt marsh pond as it looks up from hunting small fish and crabs at Merritt Island National Wildlife Refuge.*

Right: *Waves break at sunrise on the massive anastasia limestone outcrops at The Nature Conservancy's Blowing Rocks Preserve on Jupiter Island. Winter storms often hurl huge waves against the shoreline, forcing water upward through solution holes in the limestone. The resulting plumes of salt water may exceed twenty feet in height, creating the "blowing" rocks that can be seen from miles away.*

Florida are one of three areas of the coastal United States designated as critical habitat by the National Marine Fisheries Service.

Northern right whales can grow to fifty-five feet in length and weigh between forty and sixty tons. They are black in color and have a broad, flat back with no dorsal fin and a deep notch between the tail flukes. They also have two blow holes, which give them a characteristic V-shaped blow when they are viewed from the front or back. Individual whales can be identified by their unique patterns of callosities, wartlike patches on the head that are encrusted with small crustaceans.

Northern right whales are primarily coastal animals, spending their lives along the continental shelf within one hundred miles of shore. In many instances, whales were sighted within two miles of shore and were seen from the beach. They are found in the spring and early summer off the coast near Cape Cod, particularly along the Stellwagen Bank (famous for its humpback whales) and Great South Channel. By mid-summer they have traveled north to the Bay of Fundy, their primary nursery and feeding habitat. Early fall finds them on the Scotia Shelf where they gather in herds to feed and mate. Pregnant females and a few juveniles migrate to the calving area off Georgia and northern Florida to spend the winter of December through March. Adult males and the remainder of the juveniles disappear during the winter, their destination unknown.

Northern right whales and their calves face a threat similar to that of manatees—many whale injuries and deaths can be attributed to collisions with ships. Seven percent of the right whale population bears prop scars or other evidence of an accident with a ship. Mothers and calves are slow and spend a significant amount of their time at or near the surface, which makes them particularly vulnerable.

Indian River Lagoon

The Indian River Lagoon, 156 miles long, with a watershed encompassing 40 percent of Florida's east coast, is not actually a river, but rather a long, narrow estuary where salt water from the Atlantic Ocean mixes with fresh water draining from the mainland. It extends from just south of Daytona Beach to just north of West Palm Beach and contains 27 percent of the Florida's east coast salt marshes and 20 percent of the state's east coast mangrove forests. The Indian River Lagoon's more than three hundred square miles of surface water is moved more by the wind than the tide, and it does not flow from a headwaters or have a mouth like a real river. As a lagoon, it is separated from the ocean by a barrier island, and unlike other estuarine systems in Florida, there is only limited exchange of water with the open ocean through several inlets. The Indian River Lagoon estuary also includes the Mosquito Lagoon and the Banana River in its northern and central sections.

The Indian River Lagoon is considered the most biologically diverse estuary in North America, with 2,100 species of plants and more than 2,200 species of animals, including more than 700 species of fish, 310 species of birds (the most diverse bird population in North America), 68 reptiles and amphibians, and 29 mammals. Of birds, more than 125 species breed in the lagoon, while another 170 species winter there. Factoring into this diversity is the lagoon's location, which is located along the Atlantic Flyway, an important migratory "highway" for birds traveling between temperate and tropic zones. Furthermore, the lagoon's temperate to subtropical climate allows a unique mixture of temperate and tropical plants to coexist. Some 36 rare or endangered animal species live in the lagoon system. One-third of the manatees in the United States either lives in or migrates through the lagoon.

There are several major habitats in the Indian River Lagoon: seagrass, open water, mangrove forest, salt marsh, spoil island, and shoals. Seagrass is frequently found in the lagoon in vast beds, or meadows, dominated by turtle grass, manatee grass, and shoal grass. These beds offer food and shelter for young fish and provide homes for myriad creatures ranging from bacteria to blue crabs. The leaves of seagrasses, which are true aquatic plants with roots and flowers, are often covered by microscopic algae, which help the grasses convert solar energy to plant tissue. As a result of the tremendous productivity of the seagrasses, the Indian River Lagoon is known as a seagrass-based ecosystem, meaning that these species provide most of the food for animals living in the system.

Above: *Warm light floods over a salt marsh just after sunrise, Merritt Island National Wildlife Refuge.*

Left: *Resurrection ferns carpet a live oak in a maritime hammock at Canaveral National Seashore. Virtually all maritime hammocks in Florida are threatened by development.*

Right, top: *Freeze-killed black mangroves preside over a salt marsh on the Indian River Lagoon at Canaveral National Seashore. The Indian River Lagoon, 156 miles long, is considered the most biologically diverse estuary in North America, harboring 2,100 species of plants and more than 2,200 species of animals. Black mangroves at the northern end of the lagoon rarely survive beyond shrub size because of relatively frequent freezing weather.*
Right, bottom: *A full, October moon rises above the Atlantic at Canaveral National Seashore.*

Open water habitats include all of the submerged parts of the lagoon not covered by seagrass beds. These habitats include both the water column and the bottom of the lagoon, which may be mud, sand, or rock. They cover approximately 65 percent of the area of the lagoon and are the primary habitats for phytoplankton and zooplankton, microscopic plants and animals respectively, which provide food for such fish as the bay anchovy and black mullet, as well as larva of the spotted sea trout, redfish, tarpon, and other important commercial and sport fish.

Most of the salt marshes that border some 220,000 acres of the Indian River Lagoon occur from Merritt Island north, where periodic freezes limit the growth of mangroves. A natural berm restricts flooding of the lagoon's salt marshes to only the highest tides (unlike salt marshes elsewhere in Florida), limiting the plants in these marshes only to those species that can tolerate high salinity. The salt marshes of the Mosquito Lagoon are the only place in the world to find the threatened Atlantic salt marsh snake. The dusky seaside sparrow, now extinct, once thrived in the salt marshes of Merritt Island prior to impoundments for mosquito control. The impoundment of these salt marshes is believed to have

been the major cause of the disappearance of the sparrows.

Mangroves dominate the shoreline of the Indian River Lagoon south of Merritt Island, covering 40,000 acres. These forested wetlands provide roosting and nesting areas for many birds, including brown pelicans and several species of wading birds, and an estimated 80 percent of the recreational and sport fish in the lagoon spend some part of their lives in this habitat. Red mangroves dominate areas of deeper water, while black mangroves and white mangroves are found predominately in or above the average high-water line. Salt marshes and mangroves contribute vast amounts of food to the estuary, as well as help filter the water by removing sediments, excess nutrients, and pollutants from runoff before they are transported to the open waters of the lagoon. They also help protect the shoreline from erosion.

Most of the two hundred or more islands and many of the shoals in the Indian River Lagoon are manmade—the result of bottom material dredged from the lagoon in the 1950s during construction of the Intracoastal Waterway, which extends along the entire length of Florida's east coast. This bottom material, or spoil, was piled to create islands (hence the name "spoil islands"), to the detriment of seagrass beds that were either covered by spoil or died out because of the turbid water that was created.

Over the years, the islands have stabilized, with seagrasses colonizing submerged areas of the islands and trees and shrubs growing on upland portions. Mangroves fringe intertidal areas and the islands now offer roosting and nesting habitat for wading birds. The bare spoil on other parts of the islands provide important isolated nesting sites for terns and other shorebirds that normally nest on beaches, but are often disturbed by human activities. Biologists caution that new spoil islands would cause more harm to the lagoon system than would be outweighed by their possible future benefits.

Although the Indian River Lagoon is considered a relatively healthy estuarine system, it is far from pristine. In some areas of the lagoon, seagrass habitat has declined by 90 percent since the 1940s. Nitrogen levels are twice as high near areas of urban storm-water drainage and wastewater treatment plant discharge than in other parts of the lagoon. Humans have increased the historic watershed of the Indian River Lagoon by some 146 percent, significantly lowering salinity in many parts of the lagoon because of the higher influx of fresh water, to the detriment of seagrasses and several species of saltwater fish.

Records from fisheries in the late 1800s and early 1900s indicate that large catches of snook, jewfish, redfish, and even sawfish (a huge cartilaginous fish related to sharks) were quite common in the lagoon. Today, sawfish and jewfish are gone from the lagoon,

possibly because of the lower salinity. Spotted sea trout, an important game fish and commercial species, has declined dramatically since the 1950s, probably due to overfishing and loss of seagrass habitat. Based on the salinity of the water, sea trout eggs will float or sink, which can affect their distribution. Oysters, clams, and fish are also sensitive to changes in salinity, and their numbers and distribution as well are thought be linked to the wide range of salinity found throughout the lagoon.

Coastal development, excessive recreational use, pollution, and other impacts from an expanding human population negatively affect the health of the Indian River Lagoon and Florida's Atlantic Coast in general. The destruction of beachfront habitat eliminates nesting sites for shorebirds and sea turtles and jeopardizes the natural protection against wind and wave damage provided by barrier islands and their dunes to the mainland. Excessive recreational and commercial fishing can strain fish populations. Wildlife can be adversely affected and their critical habitat destroyed on beaches and the Indian River Lagoon due to improper recreational use, such as jet skiing near bird rookeries, ignoring reduced speeds for boats in manatee areas, running boats in shallow water and "prop-dredging" seagrass beds, and disturbing nesting shorebirds in posted areas. Thousands of animals, including manatees, dolphins, sea turtles, fish, and birds are killed each year after ingesting or becoming entangled in monofilament fishing line, plastic six-pack rings, plastic bags, and nets that were lost or disposed of improperly.

Our growing attraction to natural areas along coasts is creating a situation similar to that with our national parks: We are loving them to death. If we treat these areas with respect, leave them looking better than the way we found them, and are sensitive to the needs of wildlife and plants living there, Florida's Atlantic Coast will remain for future generations an enchanting, priceless landscape at the edge of the sea.

Chapter 8

The Gulf Coast

Today Renée and I kayaked with dolphins. Until the dolphins arrived, our afternoon had been fairly uneventful, taken up mostly with fishing and exploring tidal creeks and islands near the Shell Mound Unit of the Lower Suwannee National Wildlife Refuge, just north of Cedar Key. The weather was sunny and warm, with little wind, and for much of the time we just drifted on the tide, leaning back in our kayaks and soaking up the sun, stirring only when there was a need to avoid sharp oyster bars.

About an hour before sunset, as we contemplated heading back to shore, I heard something thrashing in the water close to Shell Mound about a quarter mile away. It was a sound similar to that I had heard some years ago when I had seen a pod of bottlenose dolphins feeding on a school of mullet in Florida Bay. The bay water boiled as panicked mullet leaped everywhere, with an occasional fish being flipped skyward before being gulped down by a dolphin. This time I could see no mullet, but the noise was indeed caused by a pod of several dolphins moving slowly in our direction with the incoming tide.

Facing page: *Manatees are common in estuaries on the Gulf Coast, particularly during the summer. These docile, endangered animals can reach up to thirteen feet in length and weigh well over a ton. During the spring of 1996, 158 manatees—10 percent of the Gulf Coast population—died as a result of respiratory complications caused by red tide toxin poisoning from a brown algae bloom (dinoflagelates of the genera* Gonyaulax*). (Photo © Doug Perrine)*
Above: *American oystercatchers fly through fog at the Lower Suwannee National Wildlife Refuge, north of Cedar Key. They are among the thousands of shorebirds that winter in this relatively pristine coastal wilderness.*

Dolphins roiled the water, apparently in play, their dorsal fins cutting the surface. As they moved closer, Renée and I watched a pair rise together, their noses nearly touching as they pushed their heads above water (resembling spyhopping behavior in large whales), then sinking below in unison. Suddenly, as we were easing toward the dolphins, paddling slowly and carefully so as not to disturb them, all dorsal fins disappeared. Moments later, we were surrounded by the pod.

I could see now that there were seven animals—four adults, two youngsters, and an infant in close company with its mother. They were curious and didn't seem to mind us being among them. Often they came quite close, sidling alongside our kayaks, heads cocked so that they could watch us. A couple of the adults took great pleasure in thrusting through the water beneath the boats so that we bounced on their pressure waves. This they repeated many times. We encouraged their game by paddling as fast as we could, hot on their tails as they cavorted around us. One dolphin rose under my kayak and lifted it a few inches out of the water before dropping it and surfacing beside me to gauge my reaction. I thought I could almost see the twinkle in his eye. A short time later, what may have been the same dolphin lifted Renée's boat out of the water as he passed beneath her.

For almost an hour, we stayed in the company of the dolphins as they moved through tidal creeks coursing through the salt marshes fringing the coast, some animals ranging ahead of us and at least one always lingering behind. The sun sank into the sea, burning scarlet and orange into the tortured strands of clouds that swirled without end beyond the edges of the sky. Finally, as the sunset dimmed and darkness approached, we knew we had to return to shore. Turning our kayaks, we looked back, only to see the dolphins halt at the mouth of a pass, as if waiting to see if we would follow. We were deeply touched. Not only had the dolphins accepted us among them, but they had allowed us to interact with them almost on a personal level. Never before had we been blessed with such an experience.

The Florida Gulf Coast extends from the western Panhandle south to the Ten Thousand Islands region of southwest Florida. From Cape Romano north to the Anclote Keys, and then again from Apalachicola Bay west to the Alabama border, sandy barrier islands (many with high dunes) lie parallel to the coast, providing year-round habitat to animals and plants adapted to xeric, coastal conditions, as well as nesting beaches for shorebirds such as least terns, black skimmers, and American oystercatchers.

Much of this relatively pristine coast is fringed by extensive salt marshes and offshore meadows of seagrasses, particularly in the Nature Coast region from the Cedar Keys north and west to Apalachicola Bay. South of Tampa Bay, mangrove swamps generally replace salt marshes. Several wide, shallow bays occur along the length of the Florida Gulf coast, most notably Estero Bay, Charlotte Harbor, Tampa Bay, Withlacoochee Bay, Apalachee Bay, Apalachicola Bay, and Pensacola Bay. Many of these bays form at the mouths of rivers that drain into the Gulf.

Salt Marshes

Salt marshes are productive, complex ecosystems that, like mangrove swamps, are inexorably intertwined with the rise and fall of the tide and the activities of tiny invertebrate creatures. Muddy tidal flats extend seaward from the marshes and are exposed only at low tide, when they are often overrun by a multitude of shorebirds probing the mud with slender beaks for fiddler crabs and other mud-dwelling invertebrates. As water flows out of the marshes into creeks that drain into bays, many small creatures get swept out toward the Gulf. Large fish such as sea trout, redfish, tarpon, and snook wait for these morsels to drift to them as they lie in eddies or in deeper channels. As the tide reverses and water begins to flood the oyster bars and salt marshes, fish, birds, and other predators move in with the water to feed over mud flats and in the marsh. On both tides, there is an exchange of nutrients and organisms between the salt marsh and the surrounding estuarine environment.

Oyster bars and shallow oyster shoals play a significant role in the development of many of the small islands scattered among Gulf Coast salt marshes. Longshore currents from the north deposit quartz sand near the mainland shore. As the sand accumulates, it builds up toward the surface. Given

A summer thundershower approaches a marsh filled with salt marsh mallow and hammocks of sable palm, cedars, and hardwoods at the Lower Suwannee National Wildlife Refuge.

favorable currents and unpolluted water, oysters will colonize the sand deposits, adding their limestone shells to the upward growth of the sediments. Eventually, sand and oysters accumulate to the point that they reach the intertidal zone near the surface, where the oysters are exposed at low tide.

Oyster bars are usually situated at right angles to tidal currents so that the flowing water will wash a steady supply of nutrients over them. They may become quite extensive and block wave action so that sediments drop out and accumulate enough to allow either salt marsh or dune vegetation (if close to the open sea) to begin colonizing the spit of land. Smaller, winding branches extend at intervals from the oyster bed's main line of growth, often meeting and forming small lakes and bays.

All living things in the salt marsh must be able to survive wide, irregular fluctuations in water, salinity, temperature, and dissolved oxygen. It is a rigorous environment, but food and cover is abundant for those species that can survive in it. For this reason, there are often large numbers of individual organisms in salt marshes, but the diversity of species is low.

Typical salt marsh dwellers include fiddler and squareback crabs, raccoons, mink, marsh rabbits, cotton rats, and cotton mice. Marsh periwinkles, a type of snail, festoon the blades of many salt marsh grasses. More than five hundred species of insects as well as crabs, shrimp, amphipods, and other in-

vertebrates are at the foundation level of the salt marsh food web. Birds feed and sometimes nest in salt marshes, including marsh wrens, seaside sparrows, clapper rails, various species of swallows, countless shorebirds, ducks, pelicans, and raptors such as ospreys, bald eagles, and northern harriers.

Like mangrove swamps, salt marshes are important nursery grounds for many species of animals, some of which are commercially important, such as mullet, blue crabs, oysters, and shrimp. The larval and juvenile forms of fish and shellfish feed and find refuge from predation in creeks and marshes. For example, juvenile white shrimp enter estuarine marsh creeks and remain until they are about two inches long, after which time they move to estuaries and, later, offshore to spawn. Minnows, juvenile spot, mullet, and pinfish provide prey for wading birds, including snowy egrets, great egrets, great blue herons, tricolor herons, and green herons. At high tide, redfish sometimes feed in the salt marsh, their tails thrashing the surface as they extract fiddler crabs from burrows.

Low banks of fog occasionally roll in from the Gulf, drawing a veil across oyster bars, salt marshes, and coastal islands, especially in the spring when the air may be warm, but the water is still quite cool. White pelicans, oystercatchers, willets, red knots, and other shorebirds ghost into view as I paddle my kayak near a strip of island or an oyster bar exposed by the ebbing tide, then fade into the fog as I drift past. The calls of birds fall around me like rain.

On clear days, I see bald eagles sitting in the tops of tall dead oaks a half mile away or spot a flock of lesser scaup shimmering on calm water in the distance. None of the ducks—lesser scaup, common mergansers, or hooded mergansers—ever allow me to get within a few hundred yards before they spat-

Above: *Ponds, such as this one in a pine forest on Santa Rosa Island at Gulf Islands National Seashore, provide critical fresh water for large numbers of barrier island plants and wildlife.*
Right: *A new day begins over the Cape Romano—Ten Thousand Islands Aquatic Preserve.*

ter over the water, wings thumping the thick air, until finally they are airborne. Shorebirds accommodate my curiosity more willingly, allowing me to drift within a dozen yards if I remain still. Others even permit me to quietly photograph from the kayak.

Salt marshes can be breathtakingly beautiful, particularly in the late afternoon when the warm light of the sun turns the grasses to the color of topaz. If I am lucky, a northern harrier will dip and rise above the tops of the grasses in search of small reptiles or rodents, its distinctive white rump flashing in the sun. Sometimes it just hovers as if suspended on a thread of air before swooping forward to continue on its hunt. Puffy cumulus clouds sail above a horizon bounded by islands, marsh, and an azure space of sky and water. I am insignificant in this space, but I am a part of it nonetheless.

Manatees

Although I have never seen a manatee in the Cedar Keys, I have watched them in the shallow bays that spread among the mangrove keys of the Ten Thousand Islands in southwest Florida. Once as I was paddling a canoe along the Turner River near Chokoloskee in the Ten Thousand Islands, a large manatee nearly as long as my boat rose not more

than ten feet away to loiter on the surface. I had never been this close to a manatee in the wild, and I remained motionless, hardly daring to breathe. After a few minutes, the manatee sniffed and disappeared underwater, reappearing a short while later several hundred yards away. It took a casual breath and once more slipped below the surface. I did not see it again.

Manatees are frequently seen along most of Florida's Gulf and Atlantic coasts, often entering rivers, attracted to the warmth of springs near the coast, such as those along the Homosassa and Crystal Rivers. Manatees are immense, grayish, more or less seal-shaped mammals with broad, flat, rounded tails. They share a common ancestry with the present-day elephant, hyrax, and aardvark—all of which evolved from a group of terrestrial ungulates (Perissodactyls) more than forty-five million years ago. Large adult female manatees may reach a length of nearly thirteen feet and weigh well over a ton. Their eyes are small and wide-set, and the stiff whiskers that sprout from a bulbous face give them a lovable, placid look, a bit like a walrus without tusks.

The West Indian manatee, whose range broadly extends from Florida to northern South America, belongs to the order Sirenia (named after the sirens of Greek mythology), of which there are two other species worldwide (the West African manatee and Amazonian manatee). Florida manatees are a distinct subspecies equally at home in water that is either salty or fresh.

Manatees graze more than sixty species of aquatic plants, although they rely heavily on seagrasses in bays, estuaries, and coastal rivers. They have also been documented grazing algae from the backs of their fellow manatees. They have prehensile lips and dexterous flippers, which aid them in gathering the several hundred pounds of vegetation a large manatee may consume in a single day. Because of the huge amounts of plant material they eat and the coarseness of their diet, their teeth become worn quickly. As the front teeth wear down and fall out, replacement teeth move up from the back of the mouth in a manner similar to that of elephants and kangaroos.

Manatees are gentle, long-lived creatures that survive more than thirty years in captivity and possibly live more than fifty years in the wild. They repro-

Above: *This stretch of beach on Cayo Costa, one of the most beautiful barrier islands on the lower Gulf Coast, is protected within Cayo Costa State Park and is accessible only by boat.* Facing page: *High clouds swirl at sunset from Picnic Key in the Ten Thousand Islands, Everglades National Park.*

duce slowly; a female typically gives birth to a single calf every four or five years after mating with several males. A manatee calf at birth weighs sixty to eighty pounds and may stay with its mother for two years. The first year it nurses and the second year it learns about productive feeding areas, cold weather refuges, migration routes, and other lessons it needs for survival in the wild. Unlike many other mammals, an orphaned calf may be adopted and nursed by a surrogate mother.

Manatees are extremely susceptible to cold and can be killed by a sharp drop in water temperature, possibly as a result of pneumonia or other bronchial diseases. Although they do not migrate in the true sense, they generally shift south to warmer water during the winter, holing up near springs and the outflows of power plants.

Manatees have virtually no natural enemies other than humans, from which the greatest threat is

motor boats. According to Douglas David Seifert in an article for *Ocean Realm*, more than one hundred and ninety manatees were found dead in 1994; some 25 to 30 percent of all manatee deaths are a result of being struck by a motor boat. Most adult manatees bear scars from encounters with boat propellers. Boaters need to exercise extreme caution when running in areas frequented by manatees. Many of these areas are considered "manatee zones" and are marked by signs that caution boaters to run at idle speed during certain times of the year. Given that less than two thousand manatees remain in the wild, it is essential that people heed these signs.

The Best of What is Left

Another chilling statistic brought to light in Seifert's article is that 52 percent of manatee deaths (adults and infants) may result from some combination of unknown natural causes, unknown human causes, and most important in my mind, diminished quality of habitat. Degraded and lost habitat resulting from human activities is the gravest threat facing Florida's wildlife. For shorebirds in particular, nesting habitat is increasingly limited because of heavy beachfront development and the growing use—and abuse—of beaches by humans.

Caspian terns, least terns, American oystercatchers, black skimmers, and other shorebirds depend on quiet, sandy beaches to raise their chicks. These birds are getting the best of what we have left them, and what we have left is not always pretty. In Tampa Bay, birds nest on several spoil islands that all too often are infested with fire ants and are littered with tires, plastic, and other debris. The spoil islands themselves are a product of rock and sediment dredged up from the bay bottom to create channels for large ships. On other sandy beaches, such as those on barrier islands, people and their dogs inadvertently disturb the birds and disrupt nesting activities. For example, when skimmers and their chicks are disturbed, the parents fly and family units

Sparkling bay water dramatizes the silhouette of this red mangrove near Indian Key in the Ten Thousand Islands. The crown of the mangrove is filled with double-crested cormorants, which are frequently seen on the Gulf Coast.

Above: *A full moon rises over skeleton black mangroves and exposed mud flats on Picnic Key in the Ten Thousand Islands, Everglades National Park.*
Facing page: *Wind patterns ripple the sand beneath sea oats at St. Joseph Peninsula State Park. The roots from sea oats and other dune vegetation keep the sand from blowing away. Never walk on the dunes or pick the vegetation when visiting these beautiful, but fragile formations.*

may become separated. A chick unable to find its parents may wander into the territory of another nesting pair. The adults peck at the stray chick and once it becomes bloodied, gulls will kill and eat it. Other skimmers and terns have been forced to nest near causeways that link barrier islands to the mainland, with resulting carnage of adults and chicks due to accidents with cars.

When John Muir first journeyed to Florida in 1867, he was quite moved by his first sight of the Gulf: "For nineteen years my vision was bounded by forests, but to-day, emerging from a multitude of tropical plants, I beheld the Gulf of Mexico stretching away unbounded, except by the sky. What dreams and speculative matter for thought arose as I stood on the strand, gazing out on the burnished, treeless plain!" He was also delighted by the birds, "herons white as wavetops or blue as the sky, winnowing the warm air on wide quiet wing; pelicans coming with baskets to fill, and the multitude of smaller sailors of the air, swift as swallows. . . ."

Muir's view would be somewhat more bounded these days by condominiums, hotels, and creeping developments of stilt houses that line much of the coast; the number of birds to delight his eye is somewhat diminished. I can only wonder what it was like one hundred years before his time. I try not to think what it will be like one hundred years from now. There is still much that is wild and beautiful on Florida's Gulf Coast, but for how long? This is the best that *we* have left. We must not lose this, too.

Chapter 9

The Florida Keys

To find Paradise, some say you need only make your way to the Florida Keys—a long, thin necklace of islands that drapes south from Miami's Biscayne Bay to below the tip of Florida, bounded on the north by Florida Bay and on the south by the Florida Straits, before gradually bending west into the Gulf of Mexico.

I first came to the Keys as a thirteen-year-old kid on a field trip to Seacamp/Newfound Harbor Marine Institute on Big Pine Key. It was a trip of many firsts: snorkeling over seagrass flats with schools of barracuda, finding Key deer at night with flashlights and the headlights of the institute's van (a practice no longer allowed), and swimming in the "shark pit." Those images even now are remarkably clear in my mind. I returned more than fifteen years later to begin work on a book, filled with those childhood memories, but also realizing that much had changed, and most of it was not for the better. Development, deforestation, pollution, and other human activities are taking their toll on fragile ecosystems in the Keys.

Facing page: An outgoing tide at moonrise exposes the roots of a red mangrove established on a limestone ledge, Great White Heron National Wildlife Refuge. Mangroves have the amazing ability to survive extreme conditions, including daily submersion in salt water, while growing in only the smallest dabs of mud that accumulate in crevices in limestone or oyster bars.
Above: *The setting sun sends waves of light dancing over the glassy waters surrounding the Snipe Keys in the Great White Heron National Wildlife Refuge.*

Even if somewhat diminished, the Keys remain one of the most diverse and important ecological features of North America. The only shallow-water, tropical coral reef ecosystem on the continental shelf of North America is found here, together with vast seagrass meadows, tangled mangrove forests, lush tropical hardwood hammocks, pine rocklands, and a variety of freshwater and saltwater wetlands. The tropical climate and proximity to the Gulf Stream have allowed a unique blend of West Indian and temperate plants and wildlife to colonize these rocky islands. Many species are threatened or endangered, and some are found nowhere else in the world, making the Keys an important repository of rare life forms. At less than an hour's drive from Miami, the Keys are easily accessible, a primary reason for their phenomenal popularity and a major contributing factor to their current environmental woes.

To get a first-rate introduction to the Keys, you should take to the air, preferably in a slow, single-engine plane with removable doors or windows for an unobstructed view. My first flight originated from a small airstrip on Summerland Key with Jorge "Solar George" Newberry and Bill Keogh—friend, guide, and photographer. This, they said, would teach me much about the Keys' origins and natural history. As we rose above the housing developments and finger canals that cleaved Summerland Key and banked north toward the wild backcountry of the Lower Keys, I began to see what they meant.

The day was sunny, with virtually no wind, and the calm, crystalline shallows surrounding the islands mirrored a thin thread of cumulus suspended above the Gulf of Mexico. In many places, the water was so clear I forgot that it was there, reminded only when Bill would point out the lean shadows of huge tarpon and sharks finning through channels. The backcountry waters spread before me like a sky of green, indigo, and sand; channels wended among dark clouds of seagrass meadows and emerald mangrove islands. Sometimes we would see egrets, herons, and pelicans—pale flecks in the mangroves.

From the air, the terraqueous nature of the Keys is most apparent, and I could easily see that the Keys were a world not wholly of the land or the sea. At one thousand feet, sand, seagrass, mangroves, and limestone meld into a single vital organism. Everything, it seems, is somehow linked to the tide, the mangroves, and the coral reefs.

The tide is the lifeblood of the Keys' natural environment, bringing needed nourishment and carrying away organic waste and pollutants. As it rises among the mangroves, it transports sediment, debris, and propagules (seedlings) of mangroves from other places, all of which fall out among prop roots (arching roots of red mangroves) and pneumatophores (thin, woody aeration tubes of black mangroves), continuing the process of stabilizing and expanding the shorelines of the islands. The tide, relieved of much of its load of debris and organic matter after passing through the mangroves, flows through beds of seagrass, which depend on clear water to conduct photosynthesis. Seagrass beds, densely packed with broad, flat blades of turtle grass, trap fine sediments and absorb waste before the tide reaches the coral reefs.

When the tide swirls over the coral reef, it passes through the womb of the Keys. Within the tiny limestone cup of a stony coral polyp dwells the past, present, and future of these islands. It is here that the Keys were born.

Red mangroves and a huge thunderstorm in the backcountry, National Key Deer Refuge.

Above: *Low tide exposes the oolitic ledges of Miami limestone extending from Sawyer Key toward the Barracuda Keys in the distance. These ledges are not formed from coral like many other areas in the Keys, but rather from non-biogenic calcareous particles called ooids.*

Left: *A white-spotted filefish, one of the many denizens that live on coral reefs in the Keys. (Photo © Larry Lipsky)*

Above, top: *Pine rocklands are found only in extreme south Florida and in the lower Florida Keys. They harbor thin pines, low palms, shrubby hardwoods, and a few endemic plants. Many plants are of West Indian origin and all sprout from a layer of poor soil dusted thinly over Miami oolitic limestone. This pine rockland is in the National Key Deer Refuge on Big Pine Key.*
Above, bottom: *A Key deer fawn at birth weighs just over three pounds and probably won't exceed eighty pounds as an adult. Most of the estimated three hundred Key deer live on Big Pine Key, although they also range from Johnson Key west to Sugarloaf Key.*
Right: *A thunderstorm gathers strength in the backcountry waters of the National Key Deer Refuge.*

Coral Reefs

The making of a coral reef is no small feat. A typical reef is home to many different species of coral, each living in monumental colonies containing thousands of tiny coral animals, or polyps. On the patch reefs and bank reefs of the Keys, colonies of massive stony corals and robust branching corals are crammed together, bound by encrusting organisms and the growth of corraline algae. Only the surface layer of each colony is alive, built upon the skeletal remains of hundreds of previous generations that over time have become cemented together to form the coral base rock beneath the living reef and many of the keys themselves.

Not all corals build reefs. Soft corals and gorgonians live in large colonies, but do not form protective calcareous cups and therefore do not contribute to the primary construction of the reef. Only the polyps of stony (hard) corals, such as brain corals, star corals, and the branching elkhorn and staghorn corals live in a limestone cup, an external skeleton of sorts, completed with the help of microscopic symbiotic algae called zooxanthellae, which live in their tissues. Because zooxanthellae are plants, they conduct photosynthesis, providing extra oxygen and nutrients needed by the coral polyps to produce calcium carbonate. When a polyp dies, the limestone skeleton remains as a substrate upon which other polyps can attach and grow. Without zooxanthellae, most stony corals could not build reefs.

There are two types of coral reefs in the Florida Keys—bank reefs and patch reefs. Bank reefs, which include the spectacular spur-and-groove formation at Looe Key National Marine Sanctuary, are large, diverse, elongate reefs that occur on the Atlantic side off Key Largo and from Big Pine Key to Key West. Coral development is extensive on these reefs because the land mass of the large islands blocks the flow of seasonally cold water, sediments, and nutrients through channels connecting Florida Bay and the Gulf of Mexico to the Atlantic.

Patch reefs are the most common reefs in the Dry Tortugas about sixty miles southwest of Key West and from Elliot Key to northern Key Largo. They are generally found closer to shore and in shallower water than bank reefs. Patch reefs are circular in shape and much smaller than bank reefs, ranging in diameter from ten yards to several hundred yards. Most patch reefs are encircled by a barren, sandy "halo," caused by the grazing of herbivorous reef fish in the surrounding seagrass and sedimentary habitats.

Tropical coral reefs are incredibly high in biological diversity, second only to tropical rain forests—a statistic I found easy to believe after my first time snorkeling at Looe Key National Marine Sanctuary. As I slipped into the water and angled toward the reef with slow, measured kicks of my fins, a large school of yellowtail snapper whirled about me, perhaps accustomed to receiving handouts from divers or taking advantage of the steady rain of food that must drift down from fishermen and boatloads of tourists. Below me several tarpon headed toward the open sea, gliding silently through a valley bounded by coral ramparts that rose at least thirty feet above the sand floor.

A profusion of living things occupied every cranny, every grotto, every bare bit of exposed coral rock. Sea fans and gorgonians swayed gently in the current, finding an anchorhold on coral outcrops; beneath the outcrops lingered schools of grunt. A moray eel leered from its hole in the rock, extending almost its full length before retreating, while an indigo wave of blue tang and doctorfish swirled over the reef crest and then disappeared into the valley abyss.

Taking a deep breath, I dove toward the coral, an alien vessel wallowing through blue space and a galaxy of fish. Sunlight flashed through the moving column of water like a kaleidoscope imbued with the varied hues of elkhorn coral, golden sea mat, and fire coral. I extended my hand toward a whirling eddy of tiny, brightly colored reef fish that rose almost to my fingertips and then in an instant vanished into minute crevices in the reef. It was almost too much to take in at once, and I came to the surface gasp-

Snappers and grunts swirl around elkhorn coral on Molasses Reef near Key Largo. Tropical coral reefs are second only to tropical rain forests in biological diversity, but they are extremely fragile. Pollution (including sewage, pesticides, and heavy metals), disease, boat groundings, and heavy visitation by divers and snorkelers are causing corals to die faster than they are being replaced, gradually destroying reefs that took thousands of years to develop. (Photo © Doug Perrine)

ing. Subsequent encounters with the reef have proved no less exhilarating.

Mangroves

In my mind, mangrove swamps are the kidneys of the Keys, trapping natural waste, sediments, and human refuse that would otherwise drift over the seagrass beds toward the coral reefs and beyond to the open sea. Mangrove swamps are also critical nursery, breeding, and feeding grounds for a wide variety of fish, shellfish, birds, and other wild creatures. According to information from the University of Florida Cooperative Extension Service, an estimated 75 percent of the game fish and 90 percent of the commercially important species in south Florida depend on the mangrove system.

Much of the food available to estuarine habitats in the Florida Keys and elsewhere in Florida comes from a chain of life that begins with dead mangrove leaves. Mature mangroves shed more than three tons of leaves per acre per year, adding new leaves in the process. After a dead leaf falls and has been in the water for a few weeks, the tannic acid leaches out, allowing fungi, bacteria, protozoans, and other microorganisms to colonize the leaf. Amphipods, crabs, and small herbivorous animals help the microorganisms shred the leaf into tiny pieces, speeding up decomposition. The bits of leaf and their microbial hitchhikers form detritus, which feeds clams, snails, crabs, mullet, and other animals at the base of the mangrove food chain. These in turn feed large predators, including mangrove snappers, tarpon, snook, dolphins, ospreys, and pelicans.

Mangroves comprise a loose grouping of twelve families and some fifty species of tropical, salt-tolerant trees and shrubs found on warm, low-energy (meaning little wave action) coastlines throughout the world. Three species of mangroves live in the Keys and along the coast of the southern half of Florida.

The red mangrove, unmistakable because of its arching prop roots, is the dominant tree along the seaward edge of the Keys' fringing mangrove swamps. It can grow to heights of nearly seventy feet and is considered the pioneering tree of the mangrove swamp ecosystem because of its ability to colonize a finger of rock or sand and then, once firmly rooted, build up land around it by trapping and stabilizing sediments with a spidery network of prop roots and drop roots that extend from the trunk and large upper branches. In the late summer through early fall, red mangroves produce long, thin, fleshy, green propagules, which are actually live seedlings that continue to develop on the parent tree until they are nearly eleven inches long. Then, they drop off and drift away on the tide. A red mangrove propagule can remain alive for up to a year in ocean water before it finally lodges in a sand bar or rocky shoreline, extending roots from its buried end and sprouting leaves from the exposed tip. Within twelve months, the tiny tree will develop prop roots and, with luck, continue to grow toward maturity.

The black mangrove is easily distinguished from other mangroves by its system of shallow cable roots that radiate outward from the tree, bristling with woody, vertical, fingerlike projections that poke almost eight inches above the surface of the mud. The projections, called pneumatophores, help the tree with gaseous exchange—a process not easily accomplished under water or beneath the anaerobic (oxygen-poor) mud of a mangrove swamp. The leaves of black mangroves are sometimes encrusted with salt that has collected in the dense hairs on the undersides of the leaves, giving them an overall whitish color. Black mangroves also produce propagules in the late summer and early fall, but these resemble overstuffed lima beans and cannot survive as long in water as the propagules of red mangroves. In most cases, black mangroves form the middle belt of trees, landward from red mangroves. If there are no red mangroves present, black mangroves form the outermost fringe.

The innermost zone of the fringing mangrove swamp is formed by white mangroves and buttonwoods, a salt-tolerant tree that is common in mangrove swamps, but is not a true mangrove. They occur in dry or nearly dry areas rarely flushed by the tide. White mangroves produce tiny propagules resembling peas, while buttonwoods bear a knobby, buttonlike seed case, hence the common name "buttonwood." Both trees produce their fruit in the fall.

Perhaps the most interesting ecological adapta-

Red mangrove at sunset, National Key Deer Refuge.

tion of mangroves is how they survive in a saltwater environment most plants cannot tolerate. Although mangroves grow well in fresh water, they are typically limited throughout their range to brackish and salt water areas because freshwater trees and shrubs outcompete them. Salt water, fluctuating water levels, and anaerobic sediments conspire to eliminate most freshwater plants from mangrove swamps.

Mangroves survive this triple threat to plant growth by limiting the accumulation of salt in their internal fluids. Red mangroves *exclude* salt from their system through a process that separates salt from fresh water at the root surface. Excess salt that is assimilated is stored in the leaves and then eliminated when the leaves die and fall off the tree.

Black mangroves and white mangroves *exude* salt; that is, they get rid of excess salt through special glands on the surface of their leaves. This is why the leaves of black and white mangroves are often coated with salt crystals. Although all mangroves eliminate salt from their systems, the sap is generally many times saltier than that of freshwater plants, suggesting there may be a physiological tolerance as well.

Pine Rocklands

Unlike mangrove swamps and tropical hardwood hammocks, pine rocklands in the Keys occur only in the Lower Keys, primarily Big Pine Key, Little Pine Key, Sugarloaf Key, Cudjoe Key, No Name Key, and a few other small islands in the backcountry. Few islands have permanent sources of fresh water, the primary reason for the limited distribution of these improbable forests of thin, sturdy pines, low palms, and shrubby hardwoods, all of which have sprouted from a layer of poor soil dusted thinly over Miami oolitic limestone.

Perhaps the most distinctive feature of this landscape other than the hardy stands of pine is the diverse and prolific growth of palms in the understory, particularly silver palm and brittle thatch palm. Both

of these palms are rare north of the southern tip of Florida and the Keys.

Many herbaceous plants in the understory are endemic to pinelands in the Keys, such as the Big Pine partridge pea, brown-haired snout bean, and noseburn. Other species of plants in the understory include black bead, myrsine, poisonwood, locustberry, and pisonia—testimony to the West Indian influence on the flora of the Keys. Many species of plants found in the Keys originated in the West Indies and arrived as seeds dropped by birds or borne on ocean currents or the winds of tropical storms. These species prosper because of seasonally abundant rainfall and a lack of freezing temperatures.

The pine rocklands of the National Key Deer Refuge are the stronghold of the Florida Keys' most famous denizen—the Key deer. The Key deer is a toy-sized subspecies of the Virginia whitetail, tinier even than the relatively small deer living on the Florida mainland from which it evolved. Adult males weigh approximately eighty pounds, while females average sixty-four pounds. A Key deer fawn at birth weighs just over three pounds. Most of the estimated three hundred Key deer live on Big Pine Key, although they also range from Johnson Key west to Sugarloaf Key.

Key deer are sometimes seen swimming from one island to another, especially during times of drought when they move from outlying islands to Big Pine and No Name Keys. A year-round supply of fresh water is essential to the survival of deer and other wildlife in the Lower Keys, emphasizing the importance of conserving freshwater wetlands and solution holes and limiting the consumption of fresh water by humans to protect underlying freshwater lenses (a layer of fresh water floating over a pool of heavier, brackish water in the aquifer)—the source of much of the drinking water on many of the islands, especially Big Pine Key.

Key deer move among several different habitats in search of food and shelter. In the early morning and evening, I watch them feed in open grassy areas among the pines and the mangrove fringe, as well as on the flats among red mangroves. They have an incredibly diverse diet that includes more than one hundred and sixty kinds of plants, but they favor Indian mulberry, blackbead, wild dilly, acacia, pencil flower, various grasses, the leaves of red mangrove, and the fruits of black mangrove, silver palm and brittle thatch palm.

During the heat of the day, I sometimes find them resting in deep shade near thick cover as I walk through Watson's Hammock on the National Key Deer Refuge. These backcountry deer are usually wary, snorting when they sense but cannot see me, and then finally bounding away, tails held high, when I am finally located. This is the way I prefer to watch my Key deer—in bounds and fleeting glimpses—rather than at the roadside, mugging for tourists in hope of a handout.

Tropical Hardwood Hammocks

Lush, green tropical hardwood hammocks represent the pinnacle of forest development in southern Florida and like pine rocklands are unfortunately among North America's rarest ecosystems. Most are bulldozed because they occupy high dry ground prized for development. There are a few good hammocks left on the mainland, primarily in Everglades National Park and Big Cypress National Preserve. In the Florida Keys, nearly all of the upper portion of Key Largo is protected from development in Key Largo Hammocks State Botanical Site and the Crocodile Lake National Wildlife Refuge. Lignumvitae Key State Botanical Site in the Middle Keys and some of the islands in the National Wildlife Refuges in the Lower Keys also have significant areas of hammock remaining. A patchwork of hammock remnants exists throughout the remaining keys, including the Florida Keys Land and Sea Trust's Crane Point Hammock on Key Vaca (Marathon) and The Nature Conservancy's Torchwood Hammock Preserve on Little Torch Key.

As with the plants living in pine rocklands, most species in tropical hardwood hammocks came from the West Indies, borne on the tides, the wind, or in the crops of birds. Key Largo boasts the largest, most diverse tracts of tropical hardwood hammock remaining in the Keys—a lush forest of gumbo limbo, mahogany, ironwood, Jamaica dogwood, pigeon plum, poisonwood, wild tamarind, willow bustic, and some two hundred other trees and shrubs growing from little more than bare rock. Rare life forms abound here. On the 2,700-acre Key Largo Hammocks State Botanical Site alone, more than eighty-four different plants and animals are federally protected species, including the Schaus' swallowtail and the Key Largo woodrat.

A thick, shrubby zone of sun-loving vegetation grows at the edge of most tropical hardwood hammocks, protecting the inner sanctum of the hammock from wind, salt spray, and other damaging elements. In the Everglades and other areas of the extreme south Florida mainland, tropical hardwood hammocks may be encircled by a shrub zone as well as by a moat that is somewhat deeper than the water level of the surrounding marsh or open cypress prairie. The moat and shrub zone help protect fragile hammock vegetation from the fires that occasionally sweep across the adjoining wetlands, or in many cases, pine rocklands.

The hammock relies on other mechanisms to protect itself from fire and retain moisture and nutrients. The dense canopy provides shade from the hot sun, moderating temperatures within the hammock and protecting the rich soil from a loss of moisture. Decaying leaves and twigs form a spongy layer that carpets the forest floor, providing nutrients essential to hammock plants and absorbing rain water for use by hammock vegetation and wildlife before it can percolate into the limestone bedrock. The humus layer also serves as a critical seed repository that enables a hammock to replenish itself as older trees die.

Most flowering and fruit production in tropical

hardwood species occurs during the rainy season of May through October. Late winter and early spring rains, however, stimulate flower growth and new leaf production in species such as wild tamarind, gumbo limbo, and mahogany.

Among the rare animals found in tropical hardwood hammocks are white-crowned pigeons, which range from Everglades National Park and the Florida Keys south throughout the Caribbean. These subtly beautiful birds, slate-gray with a distinctive white forehead patch, are about the size of common park pigeons and are listed as threatened throughout their range. White-crowned pigeons nest from May through September, primarily on isolated mangrove islands from Key Biscayne through the Marquesas Keys west of Key West. Most of these islands are within the boundaries of Everglades National Park in the Upper Keys and the national wildlife refuges in the Lower Keys.

National Audubon Society biologists have discovered that areas of hardwood hammock twelve acres or larger serve as critical first landing sites for young pigeons leaving their natal islands—an observation central to a conservation plan that proposes the protection of significant portions of hardwood hammock habitat along the mainline keys along U.S. 1 to be stepping stones from the pigeons' nesting keys to the larger tropical hardwood forests on Big Pine Key and Upper Key Largo.

Perhaps the most colorful creature in tropical hardwood hammocks is the *Liguus* tree snail (*Liguus fasciatus*), a snail considered by its admirers to be "the living jewel of tropical hardwood hammocks." Ranging in overall color from white to nearly black, the shells of most *Liguus* snails (or "ligs") are wrapped in multi-hued whorls of emerald green, brown, orange, yellow, or pink. Some varieties are spectacularly marked, while others are quite plain.

In the United States, these snails are found only in tropical hardwood hammocks of extreme southern Florida and the Keys. Florida's lig population is

One of three varieties of Liguus *tree snail found on Lignumvitae Key, Lignumvitae Key State Botanical Site.*

believed to have descended from individuals that may have floated over on logs from Cuba or Hispaniola, where similar snails can still be found today. From this original group of tropical immigrants, more than fifty distinctive color forms developed in the relative isolation of single hammocks or small groups of hammocks in the Everglades, Big Cypress Swamp, and the Florida Keys. Some of the color forms may now be extinct due to overcollecting and loss of habitat. Other color forms have been cross-bred by collectors and then released, potentially clouding the genetic pool of morphologically distinct and/or geographically isolated wild populations.

Ligs are generally found on smooth-barked tropical hardwoods such as wild tamarind, pigeon plum, poisonwood, mastic, myrsine, Jamaica dogwood, and bustic. I can find them throughout the year, but they are most active from May through September during southern Florida's rainy season, especially after a heavy rain when they are feeding. The snails may cover more than twenty-five feet a day as they scrape tree bark with a rasplike tongue called a radula searching for microflora such as algae, fungus, and lichens. They do not eat leaves. A snail glides along the tree bark by contracting its large foot over a thin layer of mucus secreted from special glands in the sole of the foot. The head, located at the front of the foot, sports two pairs of retractable tentacles. At the tips of the longer pair of tentacles are primitive eyes that may be able to distinguish close objects and detect the difference between light and dark. The snail uses its smaller tentacles to help it feel its way around its surroundings.

Ligs are less active during southern Florida's dry season from October through April and spend much of their time in estivation. Estivation is a dry-season hibernation during which the snails remain fastened with mucus to suitable branches. When a snail attaches itself to a branch, it seals the entrance to its shell in the process. This mucus door protects the snail from drying out. If the animal is pulled off its branch during estivation and the mucus seal is broken, it will most likely dry out and die. When warm spring rains come, rain water softens this seal, and the snails emerge from their dormant state to begin feeding. In the Florida Keys where Jamaica dogwood is common, *Liguus* tree snails may often be seen in masses along the upper branches of a large dogwood in the spring after their estivation.

Ligs are hermaphrodites, meaning every snail contains both male and female organs. When snails couple during mating in late summer, both individuals usually leave the encounter pregnant. Each pregnant snail digs a hole in the leaf litter and lays approximately fifty eggs resembling pearly peas. The eggs hatch the following spring, and tiny "button" snails emerge and begin a trek up the nearest tree to feed. Each button will add two or three whorls to its shell during its first year, one or two whorls its second year, and then perhaps one whorl each year after that until it is two inches to three inches in length. Most *Liguus* snail shells spiral to the right, but some do spiral to the left and are known as "lefties."

Currently, the *Liguus* tree snail is a listed species (species of special concern) in Florida, making it illegal to collect the shells or live snails without a permit. Insecticides and past overcollecting have put the snails at risk, but it is the destruction of tropical hardwood hammocks that has put the *Liguus* in its current precarious position. So many other animals in the Keys, including the Key Largo woodrat, the Key deer, and the Schaus' swallowtail, are faced with possible extinction as well, mainly due to the loss or degradation of habitat, pine rocklands and hammocks in particular.

This destruction is not necessary. Have we forgotten the reasons why we are enthralled by the Keys? These islands are not ours to plunder. Visitors from around the world come to the Keys primarily to explore the reefs, the hammocks, the pinelands—not the Key West bars. It makes good economic sense to practice conservation. But not everyone sees it this way.

I fail to understand the benefit of new businesses, new homes, and new cities when wildlife and wild lands are the casualties. How does this make the future of the islands more secure? The needs of people must not be considered above the welfare of the islands' natural communities and their inhabitants.

Our current thinking is leading us along a dangerous path in which nothing can survive. If we do not change our thinking, we will lose Paradise. If we lose Paradise, we will lose ourselves.

Left: *A massive strangler fig dominates its area of tropical hardwood hammock, Crocodile Lake National Wildlife Refuge, Key Largo.*
Overleaf: *Spanish moss hangs from buttonwoods in a transitional wetland on Big Pine Key. In some places around this wetland, the moss hangs like thick curtains from the upper branches of trees to the ground and must be parted in order to pass through—a deeply spiritual experience.*

Addresses

The following addresses and phone numbers are for parks, forests, refuges, and preserves that appeared in photographs in this book.

National Forests

For information about National Forests in Florida, contact:
Forest Service, U.S. Department of Agriculture
325 John Knox Road, Suite F-100
Tallahassee, FL 32303
(904) 942-9300

National Parks

Big Cypress National Preserve
HCR 61, Box 11
Ochopee, FL 34141
(941) 695-4111

Everglades National Park
40001 State Road 9336
Homestead, FL 33034-6733
(305) 242-7700

Gulf Islands National Seashore
1801 Gulf Breeze Parkway
Gulf Breeze, FL 32561
(904) 934-2600

Canaveral National Seashore
308 Julia Street
Titusville, FL 32796-3521
(407) 267-1110

National Wildlife Refuges

J. N. "Ding" Darling National Wildlife Refuge
One Wildlife Drive
Sanibel, FL 33957
(941) 472-1100

Lower Suwannee and Cedar Keys National Wildlife Refuges
16450 N.W. 31st Place
Chiefland, FL 32626
(352) 493-0238

Arthur R. Marshall Loxahatchee National Wildlife Refuge
10216 Lee Road
Boynton Beach, FL 33437
(561) 732-3684

Merritt Island National Wildlife Refuge
P.O. Box 6504
Titusville, FL 32782-6504
(407) 861-0667

Florida Keys National Wildlife Refuges, including National Key Deer, Crocodile Lake, and Great White Heron Refuges (one address for all)
P.O. Box 510
Big Pine Key, FL 33043
(305) 872-2239

Florida State Parks

For a booklet providing addresses, phone numbers, fees, and descriptions of Florida state parks, contact:
Department of Environmental Protection Park Information
Mail Station #535
3900 Commonwealth Boulevard
Tallahassee, FL 32399-3000
(904) 488-9872

National Audubon Society
Corkscrew Swamp Sanctuary
375 Sanctuary Road
Naples, FL 33964
(941) 657-3771

Ordway-Whittell Kissimmee Prairie Sanctuary
17350 N.W. 203rd Avenue
Okeechobee, FL 34972
(941) 467-8497

The Nature Conservancy
For information about preserves in Florida owned by The Nature Conservancy, contact:
The Nature Conservancy, Florida Chapter
222 S. Westmonte Drive, Suite 300
Altamonte Springs, FL 32714
(407) 682-3664

References

Audubon, Maria R. *Audubon and His Journals*. Vol. II. Freeport, NY: Books for Libraries Press, reprinted 1972.

Blount, Andrea. "Wildlife of the Prairie." *The Skimmer*, 11(3):1–8, 1995.

Brooks, William B. "Doing Right By Whales." *Florida Wildlife*, 49(4):2–5, July-August 1995.

Carr, Archie. *A Naturalist in Florida: A Celebration of Eden*. New Haven and London: Yale University Press, 1994.

Carson, Rachel. *The Edge of the Sea*. Boston: Houghton Mifflin Company, 1955.

Coleman, Richard. Personal interview with author. September 13, 1995.

Cox, J., D. Inkley, and R. Kautz. *Ecology and habitat protection needs of gopher tortoise* (Gopherus polyphemus) *populations found on lands slated for large-scale development in Florida*. Tallahassee, FL: Florida Game and Fresh Water Fish Commission, Nongame Wildlife Program Technical Report No. 4, 1987.

Davidson, Treat. "Tree Snails, Gems of the Everglades." *National Geographic* 121 (March-April 1964).

Deneen, Sally. "Who is Killing Florida's Bears, *Sunshine: The Magazine of South Florida*. No. 454:6–12, June 14, 1992.

Douglas, Marjory Stoneman. *The Everglades: River of Grass*. Marietta, GA: R. Bemis Publishing, Ltd., reprinted 1995.

Engstrom, Todd. Personal interview with author. July 25, 1995.

Fergus, Charles. *Swamp Screamer: At Large with the Florida Panther*. New York: North Point Press, 1996.

Fitzpatrick, John W., Glen E. Woolfenden, and Mark T. Kopeny. *Ecology and Development-Related Habitat Requirements of the Florida Scrub Jay* (Aphelocoma Coerulescens Coerulescens). Nongame Wildlife Program Technical Report No. 8. Tallahassee: Florida Game and Fresh Water Fish Commission, 1991.

Florida Bay Science Plan: A science planning document provided to the Interagency Working Group on Florida Bay, pamphlet, April 1994.

Florida Natural Areas Inventory and Florida Department of Natural Resources. *Guide to the Natural Communities of Florida*. Tallahassee, FL, 1990.

Folkerts, George W. "The Gulf Coast Pitcher Plant Bogs." *American Scientist*, 70(3):260–267, May-June 1982.

Franz, Richard. Personal interviews with author. July 21 and 27, 1995.

Gingerich, Dr. Jerry Lee. *Florida's Fabulous Mammals*. Tampa, FL: World Publications, 1994.

Glass-Godwin, Lenela. "Panhandle Jewels." *The Skimmer*. 8(1):1–8, 1992.

Gore, Jeff. "The Diversity of Florida's Bats." *The Skimmer*. 10(2):1–2, 1994.

Hermann, Sharon. Personal interview with author. July 26, 1995

Hoffmeister, John Edward. *Land from the Sea: The Geologic Story of South Florida*. Coral Gables, FL: University of Miami Press, 1974.

Indian River Lagoon National Estuary Program. *Indian River Lagoon: A Fragile Balance of Man and Nature*. Agency publication, N.d.

Jerome, John. "Scrub, Beautiful Scrub (Lake Wales Ridge, Florida)." *Heart of the Land: Essays on Last Great Places*. Edited by Joseph Barbato and Lisa Weinerman. New York: Pantheon Books, 1994.

Law, Beverly E. and Nancy P. Arny. *Mangroves: Florida's Coastal Trees*. Gainesville, FL: University of Florida, Cooperative Extension Service, pamphlet, N.d.

Menges, Eric S. "Habitat preferences and response to disturbance for *Dicerandra frutescens*, a Lake Wales Ridge (Florida) endemic plant." *Bulletin of the Torrey Botanical Club*. 119(3):308–313, 1992.

Moore, Julie and Carol Goodwin. *Longleaf Legacies*. Gainesville, FL: Long Needle Press, 1994.

Morrison, Joan. Personal interview with author. April 1995.

Muir, John. *A Thousand Mile Walk to the Gulf*. San Franciso: Sierra Club Books, 1916. Reprinted 1992.

Myers, Ronald L., and John J. Ewel, eds. *Ecosystems of Florida*. Orlando, FL: University Presses of Florida, 1990.

Nelson, Gil. *The Trees of Florida: A Reference and Field Guide*. Sarasota, FL: Pineapple Press, Inc., 1994.

Ripple, Jeff. *The Florida Keys: The Natural Wonders of an Island Paradise*. Stillwater, MN: Voyageur Press, 1995.

Ripple, Jeff. *Southwest Florida's Wetland Wilderness: Big Cypress Swamp and the Ten Thousand Islands*. Gainesville, FL: University Presses of Florida, 1996.

Robbins, Louise E. and Ronald L. Myers. *Seasonal Effects of Prescribed Burning in Florida: A Review*. Tallahassee, FL: Tall Timbers Research, Inc., 1992.

Seifert, Douglas David. "The Sirenian's Final Aria: The State of Florida and the State of the West Indian Manatee." *Ocean Realm*: 70–83, January 1996.

South Florida Water Management District. *Everglades: 1995 Annual Report*. West Palm Beach, FL, 1995.

Stamm, Doug. *The Springs of Florida*. Sarasota, FL: Pineapple Press, Inc., 1994.

Toops, Connie. *Everglades*. Stillwater, MN: Voyageur Press, 1989.

Van Doren, Mark, ed. *Travels of William Bartram*. New York: Dover Publications, Inc., Dover edition published 1955. Copyright 1928 by Macy-Masius, Publishers.

Walker, Steven L. and Matti P. Majorin. *Everglades: Wondrous River of Life*. Scottsdale, AZ: Camelback/Elan Venture, 1992.

Wolfe, S. H., J. A. Reidenauer, and D. B. Means. "An Ecological Characterization of the Florida Panhandle." U.S. Fish and Wildlife Service Biological Report 88(12); Minerals Management Service, OCS Study\MMS 88-0063, 1988.

Index

About the Author

Jeff Ripple, a natural history writer and photographer, grew up in south Florida and has devoted much of the last decade to exploring and photographing natural areas in Florida. His articles and photographs have appeared in such publications as *Ocean Realm, Earth, Backpacker, Birder's World, Defenders, Florida Wildlife,* Impact Photographics, and BrownTrout calendars, among others. Jeff is also the author of *Big Cypress Swamp and the Ten Thousand Islands* (University of South Carolina Press), *Florida Keys: The Natural Wonders of an Island Paradise* (Voyageur Press), *Sea Turtles* (Voyageur Press), and *Southwest Florida's Wetland Wilderness* (University Presses of Florida). Jeff, his wife Renée, and their cats Tabatha, Suwannee, and Natalie live in a small house in the woods near Gainesville, Florida.

Jeff Ripple in Everglades National Park in April 1996. (Photo by Bill Keogh)